# CONSECRATION *with*
# SHAVON
# SMITH
## A 15-DAY GUIDE OF PRAYER
## AND DEVOTION

## SHAVON SMITH

Book Cover Design: Prize Publishing House

Printed by: Prize Publishing House, LLC in the United States of America.

First printing edition 2022.

Prize Publishing House
P.O. Box 9856, Chesapeake, VA 23321
www.PrizePublishingHouse.com

ISBN (Paperback): 979-8-9858926-9-7
ISBN (E-Book): 979-8-9862969-0-6

# TABLE OF CONTENTS

# HOW DO I PRAY?

Prayer Focus - Our Love Walk To Be Strengthened

*"Whoever claims to love God yet hates a brother or sister is a liar. For whoever does not love their brother and sister, whom they have seen, cannot love God, whom they have not seen."* – (1 John 4:20, NIV)

There is no right or wrong way to pray when your heart is pure! God desires to have a relationship with you filled with open communication between the two of you!

If you desire to have more structure to your prayers, here are some helpful tips.

1. Acknowledge that you know who God is (i.e., God, You are Mighty. God, You are powerful. God, the Creator of all things).
2. Give thanks to God for all that He is and what He has done (i.e., God, I thank You for Your grace and mercy. I thank You for Your Son, Jesus).
3. Ask for the desires of your heart (make sure that your desires are in line with His desires for you).

4. Thank Him in advance for honoring your prayers because you have prayed God's will for your life.

The more you pray, the more confident you will become in talking to YOUR Father!

*"Let us, therefore, come boldly to the throne of grace, that we may obtain mercy and find grace to help in time of need."* – (Hebrews 4:16, NKJV)

—— ❦ ——

# WATCH YOUR MOUTH!!!!!!!!!!!!!!!!!!!

Prayer Focus - That Our Words Will Align With God's Words

*"Everything in the world is about to be wrapped up, so take nothing for granted. Stay wide-awake in prayer. Most of all, love each other as if your life depended on it. Love makes up for practically anything. Be quick to give a meal to the hungry, a bed to the homeless—cheerfully. Be generous with the different things God gave you, passing them around so all get in on it: if words, let it be God's words; if help, let it be God's hearty help. That way, God's bright presence will be evident in everything through Jesus, and he'll get all the credit as the One mighty in everything—encores to the end of time. Oh, yes!"* – (1 Peter 4:7-11, MSG)

- The words we speak on earth today will be judged by God in heaven.
- Our very words hold the formidable power of life and death.
- Because of the power our words possess, we need to submit even our speech to God.
- Through submission, we can experience victory through the very words we speak.

The Bible tells us our tongues have great power and influence over our lives. What we say directly impacts how our day will go. What we say can gain us new friends and get people to help us, or it can create enemies and start arguments. Once we say something, it's out there. We've said it. We can't take it back. So we as Christians had better be careful about what we say, keeping some things in check, lest we sin against God by wounding or causing problems with our words. The Bible has much to say about speaking and how we speak to others. Let's take a look at some of these ideas.

*"Don't be in any rush to become a teacher, my friends. Teaching is highly responsible work. Teachers are held to the strictest standards. And none of us is perfectly qualified. We get it wrong nearly every time we open our mouths. If you could find someone whose speech was perfectly true, you'd have a perfect person, in perfect control of life. A bit in the mouth of a horse controls the whole horse. A small rudder on a huge ship in the hands of a skilled captain sets a course in the face of the strongest winds. A word out of your mouth may seem of no account, but it can accomplish nearly anything—or destroy it! It only takes a spark, remember, to set off a forest fire. A careless or wrongly placed word out of your mouth can do that. By our speech, we can ruin the world, turn harmony to chaos, throw mud on a reputation, send the whole world up in smoke and go up in smoke with it, smoke right from the pit of hell. This is scary: You can tame a tiger, but you can't tame a tongue—it's never been done. The tongue runs wild, a wanton killer. With our tongues we bless God our Father; with the same tongues we curse the very men and women he made in his image. Curses and blessings out of the same mouth! My friends, this can't go on. A spring doesn't gush fresh water one day and brackish the next, does it? Apple trees don't bear strawberries, do they? Raspberry bushes don't bear apples, do they? You're not going to dip into a polluted mud hole and get a cup of clear, cool water, are you?"* – (James 3:1-12, MSG)

## LITTLE TONGUE, BIG IMPACT (JAMES 3)

James 3 has some famous verses on the power of the tongue. We all make mistakes often, but those who don't make mistakes with their words have reached full maturity. Like a bridled horse, they can control themselves entirely. When we bridle horses and put bits in their mouths to lead them wherever we want, we can control their whole bodies.

Consider ships: They are so large that strong winds are needed to drive them. But pilots direct their ships wherever they want with a little rudder. In the same way, even though the tongue is a small part of the body, it boasts wildly.

Think about this: "A small flame can set a whole forest on fire." (James 3:2–5, CEB)

One small comment is all it takes to start a huge argument, a fight, or a long-lasting feud. One small comment is all it takes to set off someone who's unstable. One small comment is all it takes to earn someone's enmity. One small comment is all it takes to leave a permanent wound. One small comment is all it takes to create a situation or problem where there was none. So many problems are avoidable if we can tame our tongues, if we can stop ourselves from saying what we want to say in response to verbal attacks and other provocation, and if we can keep nasty comments to ourselves. If we can find kind, constructive ways to criticize when we need to.

If we can control our speech, it will be a great benefit for us in our lives in general. We'll be making more allies than enemies. We'll be getting into fewer arguments and altercations. We'll be more successful in life because we'll have better human relationships and spend less energy on arguments and feuds. The benefits are enormous, especially over the long term. So keeping our tongue in check is not only a Christian virtue; it's a wise strategy for life!

## LET IT GO (PROVERBS 12:16, MSG)

It's a wise strategy because not every battle is worth fighting. Most arguments are pointless and gain us nothing. It's better to pick and choose our battles. When someone verbally attacks us, we should let it go if the outcome or situation doesn't matter. If we can walk away from the situation and go about our business, we should do so. It's just smarter this way. Proverbs says so.

*"Fools have short fuses and explode all too quickly; the prudent quietly shrug off insults."* – (Proverbs 12:16, MSG)

Fighting and arguments bring us down. They ruin our day, and they steal our time and energy. Not every insult needs to be answered. We don't need to dignify every insult with a response. The wise quietly shrug off insults because they know the insult will have no impact on their life in the grand scheme of things. But the consequences of getting into a fight, verbal or otherwise, could affect their life forever. If we let people trigger us with their words, they have control over us. Don't let others have that control. Learn to shrug off insults. The fight, the argument, just isn't worth it. Let's be prudent; let's be wise. Don't answer every insult.

## SPEAK TO OTHERS AS YOU WOULD HAVE THEM SPEAK TO YOU

Whenever we speak, we must never forget we're speaking to (or about) human beings created in God's image. Some lines can't be crossed, or else we sin against God. If you feel, as a Christian, that someone must be rebuked, criticized, or condemned for something, then that's fine. You should follow your conscience and say something. But be sure to say it lovingly, constantly aware of the other person's dignity as one of God's children.

## TURNING THE OTHER CHEEK

Jesus taught us to turn the other cheek, love our enemies, and pray for those who persecute us (Matthew 5:39, 44). Well, turning the other cheek is not limited to physical altercations. We need to turn the other cheek every time we're attacked, including verbal attacks. Verbal attacks include insults, slander, criticism, blame, gossip, etc. Verbal attacks hurt a lot. The sting of them can last for years, even decades. They hurt for far longer than any physical blow ever could!

Proverbs 18:21 tells us our words can cause long-lasting harm to others. It doesn't honor God to harm people like this. As Christians, we'd better watch what we say!

"Death and life are in the power of the tongue" (Proverbs 18:21, CEB). It's much easier said than done to turn the other cheek when suffering a painful verbal attack. In fact, it might be one of the hardest teachings to follow. When someone attacks us, it's our natural human instinct to fight back, defend ourselves, repay the other person in kind, blow for blow and word for word, and avenge our hurt by hurting them. It's a vicious cycle.

But all that cycle does is create more hurt in the world. When we choose to turn the other cheek, we have a chance to stop that vicious cycle. By not retaliating, we don't give anyone else a chance to retaliate against our retaliation. We don't add to the hurt in the world. It's hard for us to do because we must overcome our natural instincts to do it. But just because something is hard is no reason not to try for it. To turn the other cheek when we're the target of verbal attacks is painful. But by not responding, we choose not to add more hate or anger into the world than there already is. Turning the other cheek to words is also Christlike. We can see from His example that He didn't respond in kind when He was subjected to verbal abuse. People still slander His name now, today. He doesn't strike them down or punish them. He turns the other cheek, just like He taught us.

## TAME THE TONGUE

We must set a good example as Christians. We must practice what we preach. Since we must treat others how we want to be treated, we must treat everyone with respect. Even if they don't return the favor, we must still do it anyway — this is turning the other cheek. And shrugging off insults is a wise move. It leads to less pointless arguing.

Controlling what we say gives us great control over what happens in our life. It doesn't take much to set somebody off, so we must be careful with our comments. We must never provoke others and apologize when we harm them because verbal wounds can last for a long time. It doesn't glorify God to harm people like this. But when we feel compelled to speak out against anyone, we must never forget that we're speaking to someone God loves just as much as He loves us. Some lines cannot be crossed. We can't let anger trip us up into crossing them.

---

### SCRIPTURES ABOUT OUR WORDS

---

*"From the fruit of a man's mouth, his stomach is satisfied; he is satisfied by the yield of his lips. Death and life are in the power of the tongue, and those who love it will eat its fruits."* – (Proverbs 18:20-21, ESV)

*"For by your words, you will be acquitted, and by your words, you will be condemned."* – (Matthew 12:37, NIV)

*"When words are many, sin is unavoidable, but he who restrains his lips is wise."* – (Proverbs 10:19, BSB)

*"An evil man is trapped by his rebellious speech, but a righteous man escapes from trouble."* – (Proverbs 12:13, BSB)

*"From the fruit of his lips a man enjoys good things, but the desire of the faithless is violence. He who guards his mouth protects his life, but the one who opens his lips invites his own ruin."* – (Proverbs 13:2-3, BSB)

*"He who guards his mouth and tongue keeps his soul from distress."* – (Proverbs 21:23, BSB)

*"Tell the righteous it will be well with them, for they will enjoy the fruit of their labor."* – (Isaiah 3:10, BSB)

*"Let your conversation be always full of grace, seasoned with salt, so that you may know how to answer everyone."* – (Colossians 4:6, NIV)

# DAY 3
## CONSECRATION

—— ❧ ——

# THE POWER OF UNITY

Prayer Focus - Unity In Our Land, Family, And Marriage

*"How good and pleasant it is when God's people live together in unity!"* – (Psalm 133:1, NIV)

Unity means to bring or come together into or as if into a single unit or group. For example, the people were unified by a shared belief. Other words for unity include unify, combine, merge, fuse, and coalesce.

There is no such thing as an autonomous Christian who stands alone without the need for others and has no obligation to anyone. By definition, to be called a Christian means being a part of Christ's body, the church. Every Christian must be in fellowship with other believers and is counseled by scripture to do so.

Hebrews 10:24-25 says, *"And let us consider how to stir up one another to love and good works, not neglecting to meet together, as is the habit of some, but encouraging one another, and all the more as you see the Day drawing near."*

Six out of the ten commandments are directed toward our relationship with others, which is profound. Why would God show us how to walk in love with one another if it was perfectly fine and acceptable for us to avoid deep and meaningful relationships with other believers? He wouldn't. God desires His people to meet together, encourage each other, and love each other. In John 17:11, when Jesus prayed, *"Holy Father, keep them in Your name, which You have given me, that they may be one, even as we are one,"* He prayed for the power of unity as one body with other believers. We, joined together in fellowship with other Christians, are unified in one mission, one heart, and one spirit. As a single body, we are called to walk together toward the will of the Father. Our desire is not to please ourselves only but to please the One who reconciled us to Himself. Fellowship with other Christians is not optional for the Christian but is necessary for a healthy, biblical life.

A marriage after God recognizes the necessity for godly, biblical Christian fellowship where a husband and wife are known intimately by other believers. We become known once we let down our walls of insecurity and begin sharing with other Christian married couples what we are facing. Our struggles become known, and our sins become exposed. Through our vulnerability, other Christians can empathize with us and offer comfort, suggestions on overcoming our struggles, and exhortations on repenting and reconciling. When we become known, we feel deep concern and love from these other believers. This affirms our ability to be transparent. Our experience strips away the fears of what others would think of us and our anxieties about sharing what we face.

Jesus taught us that unity was what the Father's heart is for His people. John 15:5 says, *"I am the vine; you are the branches. Whoever abides in Me and I in him, he it is that bears much fruit, for apart from Me you can do nothing."* Jesus calls Himself a vine, and He calls us His branches, both of which are pieces of a whole. In nature, there don't exist healthy, thriving branches floating around. Instead, what is seen are healthy, thriving branches connected to the main stem of a plant or trunk of a tree, which is rooted with a strong foundation. If there are branches found in nature, disconnected and alone, it is either dead or in the process of decay. In 1 Corinthians 12:27, Paul tells us that we *are the body of Christ and individually members of it."* How can we say we are a branch if we are not growing next to other branches? How can we call ourselves members of the body of Christ if we are not connected to the other parts of that same body?

Satan will destroy your effectiveness by convincing you and your spouse to walk in complete autonomy and hide from other believers. The devil knows that believers will strike blows into his kingdom when they get together and walk together. As you walk in unity with the body of Christ in the community, you become stronger and less vulnerable to attack. We know why people avoid true biblical fellowship because we used to avoid it too. We know these types of relationships can be messy. We know the possibility and likelihood of hard, uncomfortable conversations. We know that with being known comes accountability, and with accountability comes change, which can be painful. We know that being known can seem terrifying.

However, since experiencing the power of authentic community and fellowship with the body of Christ, we have learned so much more about the good that comes from walking this way, in contrast to walking alone and isolated from the body. We know the benefits of iron sharpening iron. We know the intrinsic value of being needed and being provided for. We know the good that comes from being known, and we are no longer afraid of it. We desire this same knowledge that comes through experience to transform you and your marriage as you and your spouse walk in unity with the body of Christ. Do not be afraid of it. Do not be convinced that you can live without it. Fellowship with other believers is an incredible benefit to refining your marriage relationship. Still, it is also where you and your spouse will discover an extraordinary opportunity to serve and love others in Christ through the ministry of your marriage.

That's why we are likened to a body - because what gets things done is unity in diversity. 1 Corinthians 12:12 says, *"For just as the body is one and has many members, and all the members of the body, though many, are one body, so it is with Christ."* God stands and affirms the power of unity in getting things done. In Genesis 11:6, the Lord spoke of the power of the people of Babel, saying, *"Behold, they are one people, and they have all one language, and this is only the beginning of what they will do. And nothing that they propose to do will now be impossible for them."*

These people were united for the wrong reasons, and yet God acknowledged what ability they had. Imagine what we can do if we are united for the right reasons. That's why the first thing God did upon the establishment of the early church was give people a united language. In Acts 2:8-11, the Holy Spirit empowered the believers to speak the same language again: *"And how is it that we hear, each of us in his own native language? Parthians and Medes and Elamites and residents of Mesopotamia, Judea and Cappadocia, Pontus and Asia, Phrygia and Pamphylia, Egypt and the parts of Libya belonging to Cyrene, and visitors from Rome, both Jews and proselytes, Cretans and Arabians—we hear them telling in our own tongues the mighty works of God."*

Unity is vital to building strong and vibrant churches. Today, the body of Christ is plagued by church and denomination splits, all in the name of truth. But is the truth something that brings division within the body of believers? I believe that the truth, once centralized on the person of Jesus Christ, will bring unity, not division. The truth of God's Word should bring oneness and not categorization among us.

The enemy we fight finds no intimidation in a church fighting with one another. What threatens Satan is a force built on one foundation and brought closer together by the love of God. That's why God calls us to love one another repeatedly in scripture. He values unity, and He values relationships built within the parameters of His church. God is looking to build a church where everyone values relational unity, and we achieve that unity by being united under one banner. There is no other banner that must be lifted high in God's house than the banner of Jesus' name. There is power in being brought together in Jesus' name, and when we are united in Jesus, nothing that we propose to do will be impossible for us.

God calls His people to live in unity, so it is important to make every effort to live together in harmony with everyone. God commands us to do all in love regardless of beliefs and differences. Life is messy. Relationships are messy. Times of stress can strain relationships, and we hurt each other and destroy the unity we have worked hard for. Satan's goal is to destroy our unity. Let's fight together toward living in peace and harmony. God has given us the ability to be patient, kind, and loving through actions and words. Scriptures remind us that our responsibility as Christians is to lead the way for unity among all nations and people.

---

## SCRIPTURES ABOUT UNITY

---

*But now I want to lay out a far better way for you."* – (1 Corinthians 12:12-31, MSG)

*"I appeal to you, brothers and sisters, in the name of our Lord Jesus Christ, that all of you agree with one another in what you say and that there be no divisions among you, but that you be perfectly united in mind and thought."* – (1 Corinthians 1:10, NIV)

*"Finally, brothers and sisters, rejoice! Strive for full restoration, encourage one another, be of one mind, live in peace. And the God of love and peace will be with you."* – (2 Corinthians 13:11, NIV)

*"Finally, brothers and sisters, rejoice! Strive for full restoration, encourage one another, be of one mind, live in peace. And the God of love and peace will be with you."* – (2 Corinthians 13:11, NIV)

*"There is neither Jew nor Gentile, neither slave nor free, nor is there male and female, for you are all one in Christ Jesus."* – (Galatians 3:28, NIV)

*"By this everyone will know that you are my disciples, if you love one another."* – (John 13:25, NIV)

*"Again, truly I tell you that if two of you on earth agree about anything they ask for, it will be done for them by my Father in heaven. For where two or three gather in my name, there am I with them."* – (Matthew 18:19-20, NIV)

*"So Christ himself gave the apostles, the prophets, the evangelists, the pastors and teachers, to equip his people for works of service, so that the body of Christ may be built up until we all reach unity in the faith and in the knowledge of the Son of God and become mature, attaining to the whole measure of the fullness of Christ."* – (Ephesians 4:11-13, NIV)

*"Bear with each other and forgive one another if any of you has a grievance against someone. Forgive as the Lord forgave you. And over all these virtues put on love, which binds them all together in perfect unity."* – (Colossians 3:13-14, NIV)

*"I in them and you in me—so that they may be brought to complete unity. Then the world will know that you sent me and have loved them even as you have loved me."* – (John 17:23, NIV)

*"For by the grace given me I say to every one of you: Do not think of yourself more highly than you ought, but rather think of yourself with sober judgment, in accordance with the faith God has distributed to each of you. For just as each of us has one body with many members, and these members do not all have the same function, so in Christ we, though many, form one body, and each member belongs to all the others. We have different gifts, according to the grace given to each of us. If your gift is prophesying, then prophesy in accordance with your[a] faith; if it is serving, then serve; if it is teaching, then teach; ⁸ if it is to encourage, then give encouragement; if it is giving, then give generously; if it is to lead,[b] do it diligently; if it is to show mercy, do it cheerfully. Love must be sincere. Hate what is evil; cling to what is good. Be devoted to one another in love. Honor one another above yourselves. Never be lacking in zeal, but keep your spiritual fervor, serving the Lord. Be joyful in hope, patient in affliction, faithful in prayer. Share with the Lord's people who are in need. Practice hospitality. Bless those who persecute you; bless and do not curse. Rejoice with those who rejoice; mourn with those who mourn. Live in harmony with one another. Do not be proud, but be willing to associate with people of low position. [c] Do not be conceited.* – (Romans 12:3-16, NIV)

*"Now the whole world had one language and a common speech. As people moved eastward,[a] they found a plain in Shinar[b] and settled there. They said to each other, "Come, let's make bricks and bake them thoroughly." They used brick instead of stone, and tar for mortar. Then they said, "Come, let us build ourselves a city, with a tower that reaches to the heavens, so that we may make a name for ourselves; otherwise*

*we will be scattered over the face of the whole earth." But the Lord came down to see the city and the tower the people were building. The Lord said, "If as one people speaking the same language they have begun to do this, then nothing they plan to do will be impossible for them. Come, let us go down and confuse their language so they will not understand each other." So the Lord scattered them from there over all the earth, and they stopped building the city. That is why it was called Babel[c]—because there the Lord confused the language of the whole world. From there the Lord scattered them over the face of the whole earth." –* (Genesis 11:1-9, NIV)

# FORGIVENESS AND RELEASING OFFENSES

Prayer Focus - Give Us Hearts That Forgive; Releasing The Offenses

*"Bear with each other and forgive one another if any of you has a grievance against someone. Forgive as the Lord forgave you."* – (Colossians 3:13, NIV)

To forgive means to cancel (a debt). An offense is an annoyance or resentment brought about by a perceived insult to or disregard for oneself or one's standards or principles.

## KNOW WHAT FORGIVENESS IS AND WHY IT MATTERS

Forgiveness is about goodness and extending mercy to those who've harmed us, even if they don't "deserve" it. It is not about finding excuses for the offending person's behavior or pretending it didn't happen. Nor is there a quick formula you can follow. Forgiveness is a process with many steps that often proceed in a non-linear fashion.

But it's well worth the effort. Working on forgiveness can help us increase our self-esteem and give us a sense of inner strength and safety. It can reverse the lies we often tell ourselves when someone has hurt us deeply—lies like, I am defeated, or I'm not worthy. Forgiveness can heal us and allow us to move on in life with meaning and purpose. Forgiveness matters, and we will be its primary beneficiary.

Studies have shown that forgiving others produces substantial psychological benefits for the one who forgives. It has been shown to decrease depression, anxiety, unhealthy anger, and Post Traumatic Stress Disorder (PTSD) symptoms. But we don't just forgive to help ourselves. Forgiveness can lead to psychological healing, yes, but, in essence, it is not something about you or done for you. It is something you extend toward another person because you recognize, over time, that it is the best response to the situation.

## BECOME "FORGIVINGLY FIT"

Practicing forgiveness helps if you have worked on positively changing your inner world by learning to be what I call "forgivingly fit." Just as you would start slowly with a new physical exercise routine, it helps if you slowly build up your forgiving heart muscles, incorporating regular "workouts" into your everyday life. You can start becoming more fit by committing to do no harm—in other words, making a conscious effort not to talk disparagingly about those who've hurt you. You don't have to say good things, but it will feed the more forgiving side of your mind and heart if you refrain from talking negatively. You can also practice recognizing that every person is unique, special, and irreplaceable. It's important to cultivate this mindset of valuing our common humanity so that it becomes harder to discount someone who has harmed you as unworthy.

You can show love in small ways in everyday encounters—like smiling at a hurried grocery cashier or taking time to listen to a child. Giving love when it's unnecessary helps build the love muscle, making it easier to show compassion toward everyone. Practicing small acts of forgiveness and mercy—extending care when someone harms you—in everyday life will also help. Perhaps you can refrain from honking when someone cuts you off in traffic or hold your tongue when your spouse snaps at you and extend a hug instead. Sometimes pride and power can weaken your efforts to forgive by making you feel entitled and inflated, so you hang onto your resentment as a noble cause. Try to catch yourself when acting from that place, and choose forgiveness or mercy instead.

## ADDRESS YOUR INNER PAIN

It's important to figure out who has hurt you and how. This may seem obvious, but not every action that causes you suffering is unjust. For example, you don't need to forgive your child or spouse for being imperfect, even if their imperfections are inconvenient for you. To become clearer, you can look carefully at the people in your life—your parents, siblings, peers, spouse, coworkers, children, and even yourself—and rate how much they have hurt you. Perhaps they have exercised power over you or withheld love, or maybe they have physically harmed you. These hurts have contributed to your inner pain and need to be acknowledged. Doing this will give you an idea of who needs forgiveness in your life and provide a place to start.

There are many forms of emotional pain, but the common forms are anxiety, depression, unhealthy anger, lack of trust, self-loathing or low self-esteem, an overall pessimistic worldview, and a lack of confidence in one's ability to change. All of these harms can be addressed by forgiveness, so it's important to identify the kind of pain you are suffering from and acknowledge it. The more hurt you have incurred, the more critical it is to forgive, at least to experience emotional healing.

## DEVELOP A FORGIVING MIND THROUGH EMPATHY

Scientists have studied what happens in the brain when we think about forgiving. When people successfully imagine forgiving someone, they show increased activity in the neural circuits responsible for empathy. This tells us that empathy is connected to forgiveness and is an important step in the process.

If you examine some of the details in the life of the person who harmed you, you can often see more clearly what wounds he carries and start to develop empathy for him. First, imagine him as an innocent child, needing love and support. Did he get that from the parents? Research has shown that if an infant does not receive attention and love from primary caregivers, he will have a weak attachment, damaging trust. It may prevent him from ever getting close to others and set a trajectory of loneliness and conflict for the rest of his life.

You may be able to put an entire narrative together for the person who hurt you—from early childhood through adulthood—or imagine it from what you know. You may be able to see her physical frailties and psychological suffering and begin to understand the common humanity that you share. You may recognize her as a vulnerable person who was wounded and wounded you in return. Despite what she may have done to hurt you, you realize that she did not deserve to suffer. Recognizing that we all carry wounds in our hearts can help open the door to forgiveness.

## FIND MEANING IN YOUR SUFFERING

When we suffer a great deal, we must find meaning in what we have endured. Without seeing meaning, a person can lose a sense of purpose, leading to hopelessness and a despairing conclusion that there is no meaning to life itself. That doesn't mean we look for suffering to grow or try to find goodness in another's terrible actions. Instead, we try to see how our suffering has positively changed us. Even as one suffers, it's possible to develop short-term and sometimes long-range goals in life. Some people begin to think about how they can use their suffering to cope because they've become more resilient or brave. They may also realize that their suffering has altered their perspective regarding what is important in life, changing their long-range goals for themselves.

To find meaning is not to diminish your pain, say that you'll make the best of it, or that all things happen for a reason. You must always take care to address the woundedness in yourself and recognize the injustice of the experience, or forgiveness will be shallow.

Still, there are many ways to find meaning in our suffering. Some may choose to focus more on the world's beauty or decide to give service to others in need. Some may find meaning by speaking their truth or by strengthening their inner resolve. If I were to give one answer, it would be that we should use our suffering to become more loving and to pass that love on to others. Finding meaning, in and of itself, helps find direction in forgiveness.

## WHEN FORGIVENESS IS HARD, CALL UPON OTHER STRENGTHS

Forgiveness is always hard when we are dealing with deep injustices from others. I have known people who refuse to use the word forgiveness because it makes them angry. That's okay—we all have our timelines for when we can be merciful. But if you want to forgive and find it hard, it might help to call upon other resources.

First, remember that if you are struggling with forgiveness, that doesn't mean you're a failure at forgiveness. Forgiveness is a process that takes time, patience, and determination. Try not to be harsh on yourself, but be gentle and foster a sense of quiet within, an inner acceptance of yourself. Try to respond to yourself as you would to someone you love deeply. Surround yourself with good and wise people who support you and have the patience to allow you time to heal in your own way. Also, practice humility—not in the sense of putting yourself down, but in realizing that we are all capable of imperfection and suffering. Try to develop courage and patience in yourself to help you in the journey. Also, if you practice bearing small slights against you without lashing out, you give a gift to everyone—not only to the other person but to everyone whom that person may harm in the future because of your anger. You can help end the cycle of inflicting pain on others. If you are still finding it hard to forgive, you can choose to practice with someone easier to forgive—maybe someone who hurt you in a small way rather than deeply. Alternatively, it can be better to focus on forgiving the person at the root of your pain—maybe an abusive parent or a spouse who betrayed you. If this initial hurt impacts other parts of your life and relationships, it may be necessary to start there.

## FORGIVE YOURSELF

Most of us tend to be harder on ourselves than we are on others, and we struggle to love ourselves. If you are not feeling lovable because of your actions, you may need to work on self-forgiveness and offer to yourself what you offer to others who have hurt you: a sense of inherent worth, despite your actions.

In self-forgiveness, you honor yourself as a person, even if you are imperfect. If you've profoundly broken your standards, there is a danger of sliding into self-loathing. When this happens, you may not take good care of yourself—you might overeat, oversleep, start smoking, or engage in other forms of "self-punishment." You need to recognize this and move toward self-compassion. Soften your heart toward yourself.

After you have been able to self-forgive, you will also need to seek forgiveness from others you've harmed and right the wrongs as best as you can. It's important to be prepared for the possibility that the other person may not be ready to forgive you and practice patience and humility. But, a sincere apology, free of conditions and expectations, will go a long way toward your receiving forgiveness in the end.

## DEVELOP A FORGIVING HEART

When we overcome suffering, we gain a more mature understanding of what it means to be humble, courageous, and loving. We may be moved to create an atmosphere of forgiveness in our homes and workplaces, help others who've been harmed overcome their suffering, or protect our communities from a cycle of hatred and violence. These choices can lighten the heart and bring joy to one's life. Some people may believe that love for another who's harmed you is impossible. But, I've found that many people who forgive eventually find a way to open their hearts. If you shed bitterness and put love in its place and then repeat this with many other people, you become free to love more widely and deeply. This kind of transformation can create a legacy of love that will live long after you're gone.

## SCRIPTURES ABOUT FORGIVENESS

*"Good sense makes one slow to anger, and it is his glory to overlook an offense."* – (Proverbs 19:11, ESV)

*"Do not take to heart all the things that people say, lest you hear your servant cursing you. Your heart knows that many times you yourself have cursed others."* – (Ecclesiastes 7:21-22, ESV)

*"A brother offended is more unyielding than a strong city, and quarreling is like the bars of a castle."* – (Proverbs 18:19, ESV)

*"If your brother sins against you, go and tell him his fault, between you and him alone. If he listens to you, you have gained your brother. But if he does not listen, take one or two others along with you, that every charge may be established by the evidence of two or three witnesses. If he refuses to listen to them, tell it to the church. And if he refuses to listen even to the church, let him be to you as a Gentile and a tax collector."* – (Matthew 18:15-17, ESV)

*"Pay attention to yourselves! If your brother sins, rebuke him, and if he repents, forgive him, and if he sins against you seven times in the day, and turns to you seven times, saying, 'I repent,' you must forgive him."* – (Luke 17:3-4, ESV)

*"With all humility and gentleness, with patience, bearing with one another in love, eager to maintain the unity of the Spirit in the bond of peace."* – (Ephesians 4:2-3, ESV)

*"For where jealousy and selfish ambition exist, there will be disorder and every vile practice."* – (James 3:16, ESV)

*"There are six things that the Lord hates, seven that are an abomination to him: haughty eyes, a lying tongue, and hands that shed innocent blood, a heart that devises wicked plans, feet that make haste to run to evil, a false witness who breathes out lies, and one who sows discord among brothers."* – (Proverbs 6:16-19, ESV)

*"You shall not take vengeance or bear a grudge against the sons of your own people, but you shall love your neighbor as yourself: I am the Lord."* – (Leviticus 19:18, ESV)

*"When he was reviled, he did not revile in return; when he suffered, he did not threaten, but continued entrusting himself to him who judges justly."* – (1 Peter 2:23, ESV)

*"Judge not, that you be not judged. For with the judgment, you pronounce, you will be judged, and with the measure you use it will be measured to you. Why do you see the speck that is in your brother's eye, but do not notice the log that is in your own eye? Or how can you say to your brother, 'Let me take the speck out of your eye,' when there is the log in your own eye? You hypocrite, first take the log out of your own eye, and then you will see clearly to take the speck out of your brother's eye."* – (Matthew 7:1-5, ESV)

*"Brothers, if anyone is caught in any transgression, you who are spiritual should restore him in a spirit of gentleness. Keep watch on yourself, lest you too be tempted. Bear one another's burdens, and so fulfill the law of Christ. For if anyone thinks he is something, when he is nothing, he deceives himself."* – (Galatians 6:1-3, ESV)

*"Bearing with one another and, if one has a complaint against another, forgiving each other; as the Lord has forgiven you, so you also must forgive."* – (Colossians 3:13, ESV)

*"And if he sins against you seven times in the day, and turns to you seven times, saying, 'I repent,' you must forgive him."* – (Luke 17:4, ESV)

*"And forgive us our debts, as we also have forgiven our debtors."* – (Matthew 6:12, ESV)

*"Then Peter came up and said to him, "Lord, how often will my brother sin against me, and I forgive him? As many as seven times?" Jesus said to him, "I do not say to you seven times, but seventy times seven. "Therefore the kingdom of heaven may be compared to a king who wished to settle accounts with his servants. When he began to settle, one was brought to him who owed him ten thousand talents. And since he could not pay, his master ordered him to be sold, with his wife and children and all that he had, and payment to be made."* – (Matthew 18:21-35, ESV)

*"I have blotted out your transgressions like a cloud and your sins like mist; return to me, for I have redeemed you."* – (Isaiah 44:22, ESV)

*"But I say to you, Love your enemies and pray for those who persecute you."* – (Matthew 5:44, ESV)

*"And walk in love, as Christ loved us and gave himself up for us, a fragrant offering and sacrifice to God."* – (Ephesians 5:2, ESV)

*"Now the law came in to increase the trespass, but where sin increased, grace abounded all the more."* – (Romans 5:20, ESV)

*"And you were dead in the trespasses and sins in which you once walked, following the course of this world, following the prince of the power of the air, the spirit that is now at work in the sons of disobedience— among whom we all once lived in the passions of our flesh,*

*carrying out the desires of the body and the mind, and were by nature children of wrath, like the rest of mankind. But God, being rich in mercy, because of the great love with which he loved us, even when we were dead in our trespasses, made us alive together with Christ—by grace you have been saved.*" – (Ephesians 2:1-10, ESV)

*But if you do not forgive others their sins, your Father will not forgive your sins. Forgiveness is strong medicine for this. When life hits us hard, there is nothing as effective as forgiveness for healing deep wounds.* – (Matthew 6:15, NIV)

## DAY 5
CONSECRATION

GIVE US A DESIRE FOR TRUTH

Prayer Focus - Truth

*"I have no greater joy than to hear that my children are walking in the truth."* – (3 John 1:4, ESV)

Christ Jesus said, *"Ye shall know the truth, and the truth shall make you free"* (John 8:32). That's a wonderful promise that can be taken seriously, especially when you need some healing – whether the difficulty is injury, illness, financial hardship, a troubled relationship, or anything else.

*"The prophets prophesy lies, the priests rule by their own authority, and my people love it this way. But what will you do in the end?"* – (Jeremiah 5:31, NIV)

The Bible has much to say about truth and directly relates it to God. So how do we know the difference between objective things (broadly true or false) and relative things (true for one person or culture but not for another)?

The most common kind of relative truth is preferences. Preferences are true concerning a particular person. For example, the claim that chocolate is the best food in the world may accurately represent some people's tastes. Still, it is not an accurate representation of everyone's taste. The claim is true relative to the people with the preference. The claim may be true to a person in China, but the claim may be false to a person in India. This is what is meant by the phrase, "That's true for you, but not for me." Another example of relative truth is etiquette. It is rude to leave on your shoes in Japan when entering someone's home. In the United States, that is not necessarily the case. Therefore the statement, "It's rude to wear your shoes in someone's house," can be true in Japan but false in the United States.

The existence of absolute truth is a necessary foundation of Christianity. God didn't exactly mince words in the Bible that what He revealed were the one and only truth. In John 14:6, Jesus said, *"I am the way, the truth, and the life. No one comes to the Father except through me."*

---

## SCRIPTURES ABOUT TRUTH

---

*"I am the true vine, and my Father is the gardener. He cuts off every branch in me that bears no fruit, while every branch that does bear fruit he prunes[a] so that it will be even more fruitful. You are already clean because of the word I have spoken to you. Remain in me, as I also remain in you. No branch can bear fruit by itself; it must remain in the vine. Neither can you bear fruit unless you remain in me. "I am the vine; you are the branches. If you remain in me and I in you, you will bear much fruit; apart from me you can do nothing. If you do not remain in me, you are like a branch that is thrown away and withers; such branches are picked up, thrown into the fire and burned. If you remain in me and my words remain in you, ask whatever you wish, and it will be done for you. This is to my Father's glory, that you bear*

*much fruit, showing yourselves to be my disciples. "As the Father has loved me, so have I loved you. Now remain in my love. If you keep my commands, you will remain in my love, just as I have kept my Father's commands and remain in his love. I have told you this so that my joy may be in you and that your joy may be complete. My command is this: Love each other as I have loved you. Greater love has no one than this: to lay down one's life for one's friends. You are my friends if you do what I command. I no longer call you servants, because a servant does not know his master's business. Instead, I have called you friends, for everything that I learned from my Father I have made known to you. You did not choose me, but I chose you and appointed you so that you might go and bear fruit—fruit that will last—and so that whatever you ask in my name the Father will give you. This is my command: Love each other."* – (John 15:1-17, NIV)

*"And you will know the truth, and the truth will set you free."* – (John 8:32, ESV)

*"Sanctify them in the truth; your word is truth."* – (John 17:17, ESV)

*"The Lord is near to all who call on him, to all who call on him in truth."* – (Psalm 145:18, ESV)

*"Do your best to present yourself to God as one approved, a worker who has no need to be ashamed, rightly handling the word of truth."* – (2 Timothy 2:15, ESV)

*"Stand therefore, having fastened on the belt of truth, and having put on the breastplate of righteousness."* – (Ephesians 6:14, ESV)

*"Lying lips are an abomination to the Lord, but those who act faithfully are his delight."* – (Proverbs 12:22, ESV)

*"God is spirit, and those who worship him must worship in spirit and truth."* – (John 4:24, ESV)

*"Little children, let us not love in word or talk but in deed and in truth."* – (1 John 3:18, ESV)

*"The sum of your word is truth, and every one of your righteous rules endures forever."* – (Psalm 119:160, ESV)

*"And the Word became flesh and dwelt among us, and we have seen his glory, glory as of the only Son from the Father, full of grace and truth."* – (John 1:14, ESV)

*"Love is patient and kind; love does not envy or boast; it is not arrogant or rude. It does not insist on its own way; love is not irritable or resentful; it does not rejoice at wrongdoing, but rejoices with the truth."* – (1 Corinthians 13:4-6, ESV)

*"And you will know the truth, and the truth will set you free."* – (John 8:32, ESV)

*"Jesus said to him, "I am the way, and the truth, and the life. No one comes to the Father except through me."* – (John 14:6, ESV)

*"When the Spirit of truth comes, he will guide you into all the truth, for he will not speak on his own authority, but whatever he hears he will speak, and he will declare to you the things that are to come."* – (John 16:13, ESV)

*"Lead me in your truth and teach me, for you are the God of my salvation; for you I wait all the day long."* – (Psalm 25:5, ESV)

*"Of his own will he brought us forth by the word of truth, that we should be a kind of firstfruits of his creatures."* – (James 1:18, ESV)

*"Then Pilate said to him, "So you are a king?" Jesus answered, "You say that I am a king. For this purpose I was born and for this purpose I have come into the world—to bear witness to the truth. Everyone who is of the truth listens to my voice." Pilate said to him, "What is truth?" After he had said this, he went back outside to the Jews and told them, "I find no guilt in him."* – (John 18:37-38, ESV)

*"All Scripture is breathed out by God and profitable for teaching, for reproof, for correction, and for training in righteousness, that the man of God may be competent, equipped for every good work."* – (2 Timothy 3:16-17, ESV)

*"For the law was given through Moses; grace and truth came through Jesus Christ."* – (John 1:17, ESV)

*"Rather, speaking the truth in love, we are to grow up in every way into him who is the head, into Christ."* – (Ephesians 4:15, ESV)

*"And we know that the Son of God has come and has given us understanding, so that we may know him who is true; and we are in him who is true, in his Son Jesus Christ. He is the true God and eternal life."* – (1 John 5:20, ESV)

# COVER OUR MINDS

Prayer Focus - That Our Minds Would Be Covered

*"Set your minds on things above, not on earthly things."* – (Colossians 3:2, NIV)

A violent battle is raging around us twenty-four hours per day. The battle for your mind is vicious. The enemy will never stop his attack on our minds. It is intense. It is unrelenting, and it is unfair because Satan never plays fair. And the reason why it is so intense is that your mind is your greatest asset.

I have been able to witness the face of mental illness. I have seen men and women of all ages street walking, talking to themselves, and wandering aimlessly. I have seen what it is like when people cannot hear God because their minds are broken, and they cannot seem to connect to God even when they want to connect to God. I want you to know that whatever gets into your mind gets YOU.

Satan loves to attack our thinking when we don't protect our hearts because we often leave our minds and thoughts unguarded! It flows both ways! He can attack our hearts through our thinking and our thinking through our unguarded hearts! That's why guarding your heart and mind is so important.

Guard your mind!! Strengthen your mind and renew your mind because the battle for sin always starts in the mind. Proverbs 4:23 says, *"Keep your heart with all vigilance, for from it flow the springs of life."*

How do you guard your mind? *"Be anxious for nothing, but in everything by prayer and supplication with thanksgiving, let your requests be made known to God. And the peace of God, which surpasses all understanding, will guard your hearts and your minds in Christ Jesus."* – (Philippians 4:6-7)

2 Corinthians 10:3–5 says though we walk in the flesh, we are not waging war according to the flesh (in other words, we don't fight with armor, we don't fight with politics, we don't fight with money, we don't fight with all the humanistic ways). The weapons of our warfare are not of the flesh but have divine power to destroy strongholds. We destroy arguments and every lofty opinion raised against the knowledge of God and take every thought captive to obey Christ. The Apostle Paul says that our job in this battle is to "destroy strongholds." A stronghold is a mental block. Paul is talking about arguments set up against the knowledge of God. This is a mental battle. And he says, "Destroy these strongholds."

Take captive every thought and make it submit. Every thought must come into obedience to Christ. Make it obedient.

## KNOW THAT THE BATTLE FOR SIN ALWAYS STARTS IN THE MIND

Paul talks about this in Romans 7, saying, *"I do not do the good I want, but the evil I do not want is what I keep on doing. Wretched man that I am!"* (Romans 7:19, 24). We have so many ineffective Christians today because they do not know how to fight the battle of the mind.

## DON'T TRUST YOUR THOUGHTS

We naturally feel that if we think something, it must be true because it comes from within us. But just because you think something does not make it true. As I said above, I have seen the face of mental illness. So many different suggestions can come to mind. The world puts false suggestions in our minds, and we are bombarded with those false ideas all the time. And, of course, Satan makes suggestions all the time. But your problem is much deeper than Satan. Everybody has a mental illness. We are all mentally ill. The mental illness is called sin. And the Bible uses at least a dozen different phrases for the condition of our minds under sin. Our minds are:

- confused (Deuteronomy 28:20)
- anxious, closed (Job 17:3–4)
- evil, restless (Ecclesiastes 2:21–23)
- rash, deluded (Leviticus 5:4; Isaiah 32:4 NIV)

The Bible talks about:

- a troubled mind (2 Kings 6:11)
- a depraved mind (1 Timothy 6:5)
- a sinful mind (Romans 8:7 NIV)
- a dull mind (2 Corinthians 3:14 NIV)
- a blinded mind (2 Corinthians 4:4)
- a corrupt mind (2 Timothy 3:8)

## OUR BROKEN MINDS

Our minds are broken by sin. This means we cannot trust even what we think, ourselves. Jeremiah 17:9 says, "The heart is deceitful above all things, and desperately sick; who can understand it?" We have an amazing ability to lie to ourselves. You do it all the time. So do I. We lie.

We tell ourselves that things aren't as bad as they really are. We tell ourselves that things are better than they really are. We tell ourselves that we're doing okay when we're not doing okay. We're telling ourselves it's no big deal when it is a big deal. The Bible tells us that you cannot be trusted to tell yourself the truth. That's why you need to question your own thoughts and teach others not to believe everything they think.

Just because you get a thought doesn't mean it's correct. This is why we have so many fallen Christian leaders because all sin begins with a lie. The Bible says Satan is "the father of lies" (John 8:44). And if he can get you to believe a lie, he can get you to sin. Anytime you sin, you think that you know better than God. God has said this, but what about that? And so, you have to question what you think. 1 John 1:8 says, *"If we say we have no sin, we deceive ourselves, and the truth is not in us."* We deceive ourselves all the time.

## GUARD YOUR MIND GROM GARBAGE, GOSSIP, AND FILTH

The second thing to learn in this battle for the mind is to guard your mind against garbage. The old cliché from the early days of the computer — GIGO, garbage in/garbage out — is still true today. You will get bad results if you put insufficient data into a computer. If you put mental garbage into your mind, you will get garbage out of your life. Proverbs 15:14 says, *"A wise person is hungry for knowledge, while the fool feeds on trash."* That might be a good verse to write on a post-it note and stick on your television. And remember that the next time you think about going to a movie.

Any nutritionist will tell you that there are three kinds of food for your physical body. Brain food makes you more intelligent (food that actually makes you smarter!). There is junk food, which is simply calories — it's not poison, but empty calories. And then there are toxic foods, which are poison.

The same is true in what you see, hear, and allow into your mind. Some food is brain food. It will make you smarter, more godly, and more mature emotionally. Then there is junk food. You can fill your mind with so much that it is just stuffing. It is neither good nor bad, as 1 Corinthians 6:12 says, lawful but not helpful. In other words, some things aren't necessarily wrong but aren't necessary. The Bible tells us to fill our minds with the right things. If you want to be healthy and "successful" in the Christian life and in ministering to others, successful in your ministry, fix your mind on the right things.

By the way, some people say, "God hasn't called me to be successful. He's called me to be faithful." That's just not true. The Bible says God expects not only faithfulness but also fruitfulness. Trace it through the scriptures. *"I chose you . . . that you should go and bear fruit"* (John 15:16). Jesus cursed a fig tree because it didn't bear fruit (Matthew 21:19) — that's how vital fruitfulness is. Faithfulness is only half the equation. God expects fruitfulness as well.

Psalm 101:3 says, *"I will not set before my eyes anything that is worthless."* I know you would never invite a couple to come over to your house and ask them, "Why don't you commit an act of adultery right here in front of us?" But you do it every time you watch a TV program about adultery.

You would never invite somebody, "Why don't you murder somebody right here in my living room?" But you do it whenever you watch a TV show where somebody murders. How do you guard your mind against garbage? How do you help others guard their minds against garbage? Some people are so open-minded that their brains fall out. They think they can allow anything into their mind and will be fine. They're kidding themselves.

## TWO WAYS TO GUARD OUR MINDS

Philippians 4:6–8 gives us two ways to guard our minds against garbage: conversational prayer and concentrated focusing:

*"Do not be anxious about anything, but in everything by prayer and supplication with thanksgiving, let your requests be made known to God. And the peace of God, which surpasses all understanding, will guard your hearts and your minds in Christ Jesus. Finally, brothers, whatever is true, whatever is honorable, whatever is just, whatever is pure, whatever is lovely, whatever is commendable, if there is any excellence, if there is anything worthy of praise, think about these things."*

How do you know when you have the peace that "surpasses all understanding"? When you give up trying to understand fully why God does what He does and simply trust Him. This peace "will guard your hearts and your minds."

The first way you guard your heart and mind is "in everything" to pray. Then Paul says to think about "whatever is true, whatever is honorable, whatever is just, whatever is pure, whatever is lovely, whatever is commendable, if there is any excellence, if there is anything worthy of praise." Notice that he says to pray about everything. If you were to pray as much as you worry, you would have less to worry about. Don't worry about anything but pray about everything. This kind of prayer is like a running conversation, meaning we are not on our knees. We don't close our eyes.

I have trained myself to do this. I talk to God all the time. The average person can speak about 150 words per minute, but the average mind can understand about 350 words per minute —a 200-word per minute boredom factor. So you can certainly talk to God and talk to somebody else simultaneously. So pray about everything. Maintain a running conversation.

Second, Paul says that we should fix our thoughts. "Think about these things." How do you do that? By concentrated focusing. This is one of the keys to overcoming temptation: don't merely resist it; replace it. Whatever you merely resist persists. The more you hit a nail, the harder you drive it into the wood. And when people say I don't want to think about this, what are they doing? They are thinking about it! And whatever gets your focus gets you. James tells us that "sin, when it is fully grown, brings forth death" (James 1:15). So don't merely resist it.

## NEVER STOP LEARNING

Become a lifelong learner. Love knowledge. Love wisdom. Learn to love the act of learning. The word disciple means "learner." You cannot be a disciple of Christ without being a learner. Jesus said, "Come to me, all who labor and are heavy laden (by the way, that sounds like a felt need!), and I will give you rest. Take my yoke upon you and learn from me" (Matthew 11:28–29).

The moment you stop learning, you stop leading. The moment you stop growing, your church stops growing. The moment you stop learning, you limit yourself, and you will not be able to maximize your potential. The Bible says, *"Counsel in the heart of man is like deep water, but a man of understanding will draw it out"* (Proverbs 20:5 KJV). In other words, you can learn from anybody if you learn to draw out their knowledge. And how do you do it? You draw it out by asking questions. We all know things that others don't, and others know things of which we are ignorant. The Bible says, *"Iron sharpens iron"* (Proverbs 27:17).

If you are going to learn, you need one quality: humility. Why does God resist the proud and give grace to the humble (1 Peter 5:5)? Because the humble are teachable. The humble are submitted, and the humble are always open to receive. I would rather admit that I don't know it all than pretend I know it all and not learn. You can learn from anybody.

## SCRIPTURES ABOUT THE MIND

*"And the peace of God, which surpasses all understanding, will guard your hearts and your minds in Christ Jesus. Finally, brothers, whatever is true, whatever is honorable, whatever is just, whatever is pure, whatever is lovely, whatever is commendable, if there is any excellence, if there is anything worthy of praise, think about these things."* – (Philippians 4:7-8, ESV)

*"Do not conform to the pattern of this world but be transformed by the renewing of your mind. Then you will be able to test and approve what God's will is—his good, pleasing and perfect will."* – (Romans 12:2, NIV)

*"You will keep in perfect peace those whose minds are steadfast, because they trust in you."* – (Isaiah 26:3, NIV)

*"For though we live in the world, we do not wage war as the world does. The weapons we fight with are not the weapons of the world. On the contrary, they have divine power to demolish strongholds. We demolish arguments and every pretension that sets itself up against the knowledge of God, and we take captive every thought to make it obedient to Christ."* – (2 Corinthians 10:3-5, NIV)

*"For the Spirit God gave us does not make us timid, but gives us power, love and self-discipline."* – (2 Timothy 1:7, NIV)

## COVERING MEN! FATHERS, HUSBANDS, AND FATHERS

Prayer Focus - That God Would Cover Men

*"Have I not commanded you? Be strong and courageous. Do not be afraid; do not be discouraged, for the Lord your God will be with you wherever you go."* – (Joshua 1:9, NIV)

Men, you have been created in the image of God.

God is looking for men with humble hearts, men who will sacrifice everything for the cause of Christ and who will stand in the gap as servant-leaders for their families and Christ's Church.

Psalm 127:1 says, *"That unless the Lord builds the house, those who build, build in vain."* Prayer invites God to build His Church. My question is, are your prayers targeting the salvation, deliverance, restoration, discipleship, and leadership-multiplication of men? Praying for revival among men needs to be a contagious effort.

Healthy and growing churches are gospel-centered and intentional about building men. Do we see an ever-increasing company of men being added to our church because they heard the gospel, believed its message, and were saved?

How are we engaging lost men in our community and leading them to Christ? The goal is to teach men to obey the commands of Jesus to grow spiritually. Building men in the faith involves teaching the Bible basics and practical, transferable concepts for being a self-feeder in the Word. The third discipleship phase is "sending." The goal is for a man to discover his spiritual gifts, develop a heart for evangelism, and be empowered to reproduce himself spiritually.

Men must be called and equipped to be spiritual leaders if the church is ever going to fulfill the Great Commission, if our families are ever going to be healthy, and if our children will be good citizens and successful in this life. The Church is the world's hope, and men are the church's hope. God is looking for men. God is looking for you. Will you be like Isaiah in Isaiah 6:8 and say to the Lord, "Here am I, send me!"

Ezekiel 22:30 says, *"I searched for a man among them who would build up the wall and stand in the gap before Me for the land that I might not destroy it, but I found no one."*

---

## SCRIPTURES CONCERNING MAN

*"Be watchful, stand firm in the faith, act like men, be strong. Let all that you do be done in love."* – (1 Corinthians 16:13-14, ESV)

*"Blessed is the man who walks not in the counsel of the wicked, nor stands in the way of sinners, nor sits in the seat of scoffers; but his delight is in the law of the Lord, and on his law he meditates day and night. He is like a tree planted by streams of water that yields its fruit in its season, and its leaf does not wither. In all that he does, he prospers.*

*The wicked are not so, but are like chaff that the wind drives away. Therefore, the wicked will not stand in the judgment, nor sinners in the congregation of the righteous."* – (Psalm 1:1-6, ESV)

*"Show yourself in all respects to be a model of good works, and in your teaching show integrity, dignity."* – (Titus 2:7, ESV)

*"When I was a child, I spoke like a child, I thought like a child, I reasoned like a child. When I became a man, I gave up childish ways."* – (1 Corinthians 13:11, ESV)

*"How can a young man keep his way pure? By guarding it according to your word. With my whole heart I seek you; let me not wander from your commandments! I have stored up your word in my heart, that I might not sin against you. Blessed are you, O Lord; teach me your statutes! With my lips I declare all the rules of your mouth."* – (Psalm 119:9-16, ESV)

*"But if anyone does not provide for his relatives, and especially for members of his household, he has denied the faith and is worse than an unbeliever."* – (1 Timothy 5:8, ESV)

*"But as for you, O man of God, flee these things. Pursue righteousness, godliness, faith, love, steadfastness, gentleness."* – (1 Timothy 6:11, ESV)

*"The steps of a man are established by the Lord, when he delights in his way."* – (Psalm 37:23, ESV)

*"Wives, submit to your own husbands, as to the Lord. For the husband is the head of the wife even as Christ is the head of the church, his body, and is himself its Savior. Now as the church submits to Christ, so also*

*wives should submit in everything to their husbands. Husbands, love your wives, as Christ loved the church and gave himself up for her." –* (Ephesians 5:22-25, ESV)

*"Praise the Lord! Blessed is the man who fears the Lord, who greatly delights in his commandments! His offspring will be mighty in the land; the generation of the upright will be blessed. Wealth and riches are in his house, and his righteousness endures forever. Light dawns in the darkness for the upright; he is gracious, merciful, and righteous. It is well with the man who deals generously and lends; who conducts his affairs with justice." –* (Psalm 112:1-10, ESV)

*"Do you see a man skillful in his work? He will stand before kings; he will not stand before obscure men." –* (Proverbs 22:29, ESV)

*"Then God said, "Let us make man in our image, after our likeness. And let them have dominion over the fish of the sea and over the birds of the heavens and over the livestock and over all the earth and over every creeping thing that creeps on the earth." –* (Genesis 1:26, ESV)

*"Fathers, do not provoke your children to anger, but bring them up in the discipline and instruction of the Lord." –* (Ephesians 6:4, ESV)

*"Therefore, a man shall leave his father and his mother and hold fast to his wife, and they shall become one flesh." –* (Genesis 2:24, ESV)

*"And the angel of the Lord appeared to him and said to him, "The Lord is with you, O mighty man of valor." –* (Judges 6:12, ESV)

*"Then the Lord God said, "It is not good that the man should be alone; I will make him a helper fit for him." –* (Genesis 2:18, ESV)

*"The end of the matter; all has been heard. Fear God and keep his commandments, for this is the whole duty of man."* – (Ecclesiastes 12:13, ESV)

*"Husbands, love your wives, as Christ loved the church and gave himself up for her."* – (Ephesians 5:25, ESV)

*"And what you have heard from me in the presence of many witnesses entrust to faithful men who will be able to teach others also."* – (2 Timothy 2:2, ESV)

*"All Scripture is breathed out by God and profitable for teaching, for reproof, for correction, and for training in righteousness."* – (2 Timothy 3:16, ESV)

*"Husbands, love your wives, and do not be harsh with them."* – (Colossians 3:19, ESV)

*"The Lord God took the man and put him in the garden of Eden to work it and keep it."* – (Genesis 2:15, ESV)

*"And he humbled you and let you hunger and fed you with manna, which you did not know, nor did your fathers know, that he might make you know that man does not live by bread alone, but man lives by every word that comes from the mouth of the Lord."* – (Deuteronomy 8:3, ESV)

*"I am about to go the way of all the earth. Be strong and show yourself a man."* – (1 Kings 2:2, ESV)

*"For the husband is the head of the wife even as Christ is the head of the church, his body, and is himself its Savior."* – (Ephesians 5:23, ESV)

*"He who finds a wife finds a good thing and obtains favor from the Lord."* – (Proverbs 18:22, ESV)

*"Or do you not know that the unrighteous will not inherit the kingdom of God? Do not be deceived: neither the sexually immoral, nor idolaters, nor adulterers, nor men who practice homosexuality, nor thieves, nor the greedy, nor drunkards, nor revilers, nor swindlers will inherit the kingdom of God."* – (1 Corinthians 6:9-10, ESV)

*"Keep your heart with all vigilance, for from it flow the springs of life."* – (Proverbs 4:23, ESV)

*"A fool gives full vent to his spirit, but a wise man quietly holds it back."* – (Proverbs 29:11, ESV)

# COVERING WOMEN, MOTHERS AND WIVES

Prayer Focus - That God Would Cover Women

*"God is within her; she will not fall; God will help her at break of day."* – (Psalm 46:5)

Mary's significant role in scripture is widely known. Mary of Nazareth is the mother of Jesus. She gave birth to the Savior of the world when she was just a teenager. The angel Gabriel told her of the unique role she would play in God's story, and while this certainly was frightening, Mary bravely embraced her calling and bore for all of humanity the savior of the world.

What you are carrying is going to cost you everything!

Mary was willing to be humiliated.
Mary was willing to lose her fiancé.
Mary was willing to be ostracized.

God used an ordinary person to do something extraordinary. Mary never gave all her reasons for why she didn't qualify. She accepted the will of God. You are carrying something bigger than you! You are a carrier of destiny. You are a carrier of a world changer.

## STORY OF JEZEBEL AND AHAB

*"Sometime later there was an incident involving a vineyard belonging to Naboth the Jezreelite. The vineyard was in Jezreel, close to the palace of Ahab king of Samaria. Ahab said to Naboth, "Let me have your vineyard to use for a vegetable garden, since it is close to my palace. In exchange I will give you a better vineyard or, if you prefer, I will pay you whatever it is worth." But Naboth replied, "The Lord forbid that I should give you the inheritance of my ancestors." So Ahab went home, sullen and angry because Naboth the Jezreelite had said, "I will not give you the inheritance of my ancestors." He lay on his bed sulking and refused to eat. His wife Jezebel came in and asked him, "Why are you so sullen? Why won't you eat?" He answered her, "Because I said to Naboth the Jezreelite, 'Sell me your vineyard; or if you prefer, I will give you another vineyard in its place.' But he said, 'I will not give you my vineyard.'" Jezebel his wife said, "Is this how you act as king over Israel? Get up and eat! Cheer up. I'll get you the vineyard of Naboth the Jezreelite." So, she wrote letters in Ahab's name, placed his seal on them, and sent them to the elders and nobles who lived in Naboth's city with him. In those letters she wrote: "Proclaim a day of fasting and seat Naboth in a prominent place among the people. But seat two scoundrels opposite him and have them bring charges that he has cursed both God and the king. Then take him out and stone him to death." So the elders and nobles who lived in Naboth's city did as Jezebel directed in the letters she had written to them. They proclaimed a fast and seated Naboth in a prominent place among the people. Then two scoundrels came and sat opposite him and brought charges against Naboth before the people, saying, "Naboth has cursed both God and the king." So they took him outside the city and*

*stoned him to death. Then they sent word to Jezebel: "Naboth has been stoned to death." As soon as Jezebel heard that Naboth had been stoned to death, she said to Ahab, "Get up and take possession of the vineyard of Naboth the Jezreelite that he refused to sell you. He is no longer alive, but dead." When Ahab heard that Naboth was dead, he got up and went down to take possession of Naboth's vineyard. Then the word of the Lord came to Elijah the Tishbite: "Go down to meet Ahab king of Israel, who rules in Samaria. He is now in Naboth's vineyard, where he has gone to take possession of it. Say to him, 'This is what the Lord says: Have you not murdered a man and seized his property?' Then say to him, 'This is what the Lord says: In the place where dogs licked up Naboth's blood, dogs will lick up your blood—yes, yours!'"*

*Ahab said to Elijah, "So you have found me, my enemy!" "I have found you," he answered, "because you have sold yourself to do evil in the eyes of the Lord. He says, 'I am going to bring disaster on you. I will wipe out your descendants and cut off from Ahab every last male in Israel—slave or free. I will make your house like that of Jeroboam son of Nebat and that of Baasha son of Ahijah, because you have aroused my anger and have caused Israel to sin.'*

*"And also concerning Jezebel the Lord says: 'Dogs will devour Jezebel by the wall of Jezreel.'*

*"Dogs will eat those belonging to Ahab who die in the city, and the birds will feed on those who die in the country." (There was never anyone like Ahab, who sold himself to do evil in the eyes of the Lord, urged on by Jezebel his wife. He behaved in the vilest manner by going after idols, like the Amorites the Lord drove out before Israel.) When Ahab heard these words, he tore his clothes, put on sackcloth and fasted. He lay in sackcloth and went around meekly. Then the word of the Lord came to Elijah the Tishbite: "Have you noticed how Ahab has humbled himself before me? Because he has humbled himself, I will not bring this disaster in his day, but I will bring it on his house in the days of his son." – (1 Kings 21: 1-28, NIV)*

## SCRIPTURES CONCERNING WOMEN

*"Older women likewise are to be reverent in behavior, not slanderers or slaves to much wine. They are to teach what is good, and so train the young women to love their husbands and children, to be self-controlled, pure, working at home, kind, and submissive to their own husbands, that the word of God may not be reviled."* – (Titus 2:3-5, ESV)

*"The wisest of women builds her house, but folly with her own hands tears it down."* – (Proverbs 14:1, ESV)

*"A gracious woman gets honor, and violent men get riches."* – (Proverbs 11:16, ESV)

*"She opens her mouth with wisdom, and the teaching of kindness is on her tongue."* – (Proverbs 31:26, ESV)

*"Charm is deceitful, and beauty is vain, but a woman who fears the Lord is to be praised."* – (Proverbs 31:30, ESV)

*"It is better to live in a corner of the housetop than in a house shared with a quarrelsome wife."* – (Proverbs 21:9, ESV)

*"An excellent wife is the crown of her husband, but she who brings shame is like rottenness in his bones."* – (Proverbs 12:4, ESV)

*"Charm is deceitful, and beauty is vain, but a woman who fears the Lord is to be praised. Give her of the fruit of her hands, and let her works praise her in the gates."* – (Proverbs 31:30-31, ESV)

*"It is not good for the man to be alone. I will make a helper [ezer] suitable for him."* – (Genesis 2:18, ESV) (Hebrew word God used when creating Eve: the ezer. An agent of rescue suitable for him!)

# COVERING OUR CHILDREN

Prayer Focus - That God Would Cover Children

*"All your children will be taught by the Lord, and great will be their peace."* – (Isaiah 54:13, NIV)

## 1. NEGLECTING TIME WITH OUR CHILDREN

Teaching them will require quality time.

*"You shall teach them diligently to your children and shall talk of them when you sit in your house, and when you walk by the way, and when you lie down, and when you rise. You shall bind them as a sign on your hand, and they shall be as frontlets between your eyes."* – (Deuteronomy 6:7–8)

God wants us to spend purposeful, quality time with our children. We need time to talk with our children and give them wise instructions. We need enough time with our children to model godly living. Teaching our children requires time to show them how to live out the ordinary moments.

Spending time with our children involves ordinary moments.

When we ignore our children, we forfeit an important responsibility. They will look to other people to be their surrogate parents. They will begin to harbor bitterness. Don't encourage your children to get angry with you. Don't neglect them.

## 2. CONSISTENT ANGER AND FRUSTRATION

*"Make no friendship with a man given to anger, nor go with a wrathful man, lest you learn his ways and entangle yourself in a snare."* – (Proverbs 22:24–25)

People are impressionable, especially children. Here are several things our kids learn when they see us get angry.

- They learn incorrectly that God tolerates sinful anger. "If mom and dad get angry, it must be ok to God."
- They learn incorrectly that sinful anger is justifiable in certain situations. "If mom and dad get angry, it must be appropriate in certain situations."
- They learn incorrectly that sinful anger is inevitable. "If mom and dad get angry daily, it cannot be avoided."
- They learn incorrectly that sinful anger is necessary to help them get what they want. "If mom and dad get angry to get what they want, I can get angry to get what I want."

It is unrealistic to expect our children to "do as I say, not as I do." To avoid provoking our children is not our foremost motivation to control our anger. We restrain our sinful anger in obedience to God because we love God. Our motivation is Christ. We love God, and therefore we obey God's commands. We provoke our children to anger when we get angry. Resolve to mortify your sinful anger today.

## 3. TALKING TO OUR CHILDREN HARSHLY

*"O LORD, rebuke me not in your anger, nor discipline me in your wrath!"* – (Psalm 38:1)

*"Let no corrupting talk come out of your mouths, but only such as is good for building up, as fits the occasion, that it may give grace to those who hear."* – (Ephesians 4:29)

Calling them names, making them feel unqualified and less than! What is worse than getting sinfully angry? So before you discipline your children, ask three questions.

*Question 1: Am I Disciplining My Child for a Specific Sinful Action?*
You should be able to name the rule that your child has broken. This may be a specific biblical command, or it may be a personal house rule.

Ultimately, I want to correct my child's heart. But unless my child can articulate the sins they have committed or the mistakes they have made, I cannot judge their thoughts and intentions.

*Question 2: Am I Disciplining My Child Because He Offended God?*
We are responsible for correcting our children, but we must correct them with the proper motivation. We do not discipline our children because we have been offended. If that is our heart posture, we will discipline with harshness and anger. We discipline our children because they have offended God. We want our children to honor God. Our creator God makes the rules. If we break God's rules, there is a penalty. Discipline is to reinforce this reality.

*Question 3: Am I Disciplining My Child with the Gospel of Jesus Christ in Mind?*
Even though I am a Christian, I still break God's rules. We must be honest with our children and remind them that we cannot meet God's standard in our own strength. We should share with them

moments where we have struggled and failed, but with the strength of God, we overcame. We cannot obey God without His enablement. It is important to persevere in our sanctification process, but we must understand that we also need God's grace, mercy, and forgiveness. Avoid scolding harshly and with an angry spirit; but instead, discipline appropriately. It requires the right occasion, manner, and motivation. It is better to forsake discipline than to discipline in anger.

## 4. FIND FAULT WITH OUR CHILDREN CONSTANTLY

*"He burned with anger also at Job's three friends because they had found no answer, although they had declared Job to be in the wrong."* – (Job 32:3)

Do you get hurt when a friend finds fault with you? That is how your children feel when you find unnecessary fault in your children.

When you convey this type of message, your children feel hurt. They get sad. They get depressed. And then, they get angry. Don't find unnecessary fault in your children. Love them for who they are and love their faults and imperfections. Remember that God loves us despite our imperfections. We can love with Christ as our model and motivation.

## 5. REFUSE TO LISTEN TO OUR CHILDREN

*"If one gives an answer before he hears, it is his folly and shame."* – (Proverbs 18:13)

All of us want to be heard. We want someone to listen to us and understand us. We want to plead our case. We desire an opportunity to persuade, even if we do not get our way. Our children want the same thing. They want people to listen to them, especially their moms and dads.

I'm not saying we cannot tell our children that "now is not a good time," but if we do not actively listen to them, they will be disappointed; if we persist in ignoring them, they will get resentful and angry.

## 6. PERMIT OUR CHILDREN TOO MUCH

*"The rod and reproof give wisdom, but a child left to himself brings shame to his mother." –* (Proverbs 29:15)

*"I mean that the heir, as long as he is a child, is no different from a slave, though he is the owner of everything, but he is under guardians and managers until the date set by his father." –* (Galatians 4:1–2)

Don't be afraid to set proper rules and boundaries for your children. Children do not have their parent's wisdom. Children need protection. They need parameters. Freedom and liberty are coveted in our society. We want a choice. We want options. But giving your children too many choices can brew frustration and anger.

Our children should learn that they cannot get everything they want at an early age. They must learn how to submit to authority, and submission occurs when they comply with doing something against their preference.

Parents who set parameters and enforce structure and discipline love their children. Children learn that parents who permit much love little. Do not permit your children too much.

## 7. DEMAND TOO MUCH FROM OUR CHILDREN

*"But the wisdom from above is first pure, then peaceable, gentle, open to reason, full of mercy and good fruits, impartial and sincere." –* (James 3:17)

*"When I was a child, I spoke like a child, I thought like a child, I reasoned like a child. When I became a man, I gave up childish ways." –* (1 Corinthians 13:11)

Every child is different. As parents, we need to exercise wisdom with our children when we place demands on them. Our expectations must be reasonable. Do not demand too much. When we demand too much from our children, we foster resentment. They may suppress it for a while, but they may explode in anger one day.

## 8. SET DOUBLE STANDARDS OR CHANGING STANDARDS

*"Was I vacillating when I wanted to do this? Do I make my plans according to the flesh, ready to say "Yes, yes" and "No, no" at the same time? As surely as God is faithful, our word to you has not been Yes and No." –* (2 Corinthians 1:17–18)

*"He is a double-minded man, unstable in all his ways." –* (James 1:8)

We gain our children's trust when we are consistent. When we change the rules or apply our rules inconsistently, our children get confused. We appear undependable. This creates unease, and our children get frustrated. When parents are inconsistent, children get frustrated. Don't change your standards, rules, and expectations. Make sure you and your spouse are always on the same page regarding disciplining our children.

## 9. COMPARE OUR CHILDREN TO OTHERS

*"Not that we dare to classify or compare ourselves with some of those who are commending themselves. But when they measure themselves by one another and compare themselves with one another, they are without understanding." –* (2 Corinthians 10:12)

"Why can't you be more like...?" That is probably one of the most hurtful things we can say to another person. Our children receive that message when we compare them with others. Each of us is unique. God created us with different strengths and weaknesses. We maximize our strengths while limiting the significance of our weaknesses.

When we compare our children to others, we are telling them that we are not satisfied with how God created them. Slowly they become discouraged with who they are. This leads to a downward spiral as our children grow in animosity.

We want good role models both for ourselves and our children. Seeking godly examples is wise. Paul exhorted Christians to imitate him as he imitates Christ.

Children want their parents to be proud of them. They want to hear the words, "Good job." If you commend another child more than your own, you will cultivate ill feelings in your children. Focus on your children's strengths and virtues. Compliment your children. Encourage them. Remind them that they are special and they are loved.

## 10. BREAK OUR PROMISES

*"Let what you say be simply 'Yes' or 'No'; anything more than this comes from evil."* – (Matthew 5:37)

*"Do not lie to one another, seeing that you have put off the old self with its practices."* – (Colossians 3:9)

Disappointments can be detrimental to your children. Do not break your promises to them. If you have promised them something and cannot fulfill it, sit them down to explain why, but also let them know that you will make it up to them. Repeatedly breaking promises decreases your children's confidence in you.

## 11. CHASTEN OUR CHILDREN IN PUBLIC

*"If your brother sins against you, go and tell him his fault, between you and him alone. If he listens to you, you have gained your brother."* – (Matthew 18:15)

It dishonors God and our children when we correct them before others. God wants us to reprimand in private. Correction in private shows kindness, consideration, and respect. When we announce our children's wrongdoing to everyone, we shame our children. They feel ridiculed and scorned. Then, they get angry.

## 12. SHOW FAVORITISM

*"But he answered his father, 'Look, these many years I have served you, and I never disobeyed your command, yet you never gave me a young goat, that I might celebrate with my friends."* – (Luke 15:29)

*"My brothers, show no partiality as you hold the faith in our Lord Jesus Christ, the Lord of glory."* – (James 2:1)

Don't be quick to think you are blameless with God's command in Ephesians 6:4. We provoke our children to anger in many subtle ways. Nevertheless, God forgives us and gives us daily grace to raise our children in godly discipline and instruction. Be quick to ask your children for forgiveness. Be gracious with your children. Look for ways that you are provoking your children to anger. You might be surprised what you find.

### SCRIPTURES CONCERNING CHILDREN

*"Children are a heritage from the Lord, offspring a reward from him. Like arrows in the hands of a warrior are children born in one's youth. Blessed is the man whose quiver is full of them. They will not be put*

*to shame when they contend with their opponents in court." –* (Psalm 127:3-5, NIV)

*"Fathers do not provoke your children to anger by the way you treat them. Rather, bring them up with the discipline and instruction that comes from the Lord." –* (Ephesians 6:4, NLT)

# PRAYERS FOR HEALING OF SICKNESS... MENTAL, EMOTIONAL AND PHYSICAL

Prayer Focus - That God Would Heal

*"Is anyone among you sick? Let them call the elders of the church to pray over them and anoint them with oil in the name of the Lord. And the prayer offered in faith will make the sick person well; the Lord will raise them up. If they have sinned, they will be forgiven. Therefore, confess your sins to each other and pray for each other so that you may be healed. The prayer of a righteous person is powerful and effective."* – (James 5:14-16, NIV)

## THERE ARE PHYSICAL AND SPIRITUAL CAUSES FOR SICKNESS

Scripture speaks of both physical and spiritual causes for sickness. Sometimes a person is ill for merely physical reasons, while at other times, there are spiritual factors that are the cause of the sickness.

When we examine the Bible, we find that sickness can have a natural origin or supernatural. It is not always natural, nor is the origin of sickness always supernatural. We must understand this important truth.

## SICKNESS CAN COME AS A RESULT OF BREAKING GOD'S LAWS

There are times when people get sick simply because they violate the laws that God has established. For example, if we do not take care of our bodies, we risk ourselves becoming ill. Indeed, we find that God gave the nation Israel specific laws to follow while they were traveling in the wilderness toward the Promised Land. These laws not only had ceremonial value but were also given for the continued health of the people. If the people of Israel violated these laws, then illness could result.

## SICKNESS ITSELF IS NOT SIN

I want to emphasize that the Bible does not equate sickness with sin. This is illustrated in an episode in the life of Jesus. As he went along, He saw a man blind from birth. His disciples asked Him, "Rabbi, who sinned, this man or his parents, that he was born blind?" "Neither this man nor his parents sinned," said Jesus, "but this happened so that the work of God might be displayed in his life" (John 9:1-3, NIV).

Jesus' disciples assumed that this man was blind because of some sin he or his parents may have committed. However, in this case, Jesus taught otherwise. His blindness was going to result in the glory of God. Indeed, Jesus miraculously healed this man giving him sight for the first time in his life. Thus, it was not his sin that caused his blindness.

Nobody in scripture was ever judged because they were sick. They were judged because they were sinful.

## SICKNESS CAN BE THE RESULT OF SIN

While sickness is not sin, sickness can be the result of sin. Paul emphasized that our body is the temple of the Holy Spirit. He wrote the following to the Corinthians.

*"Or do you not know that your body is a temple of the Holy Spirit within you, which you have from God, and that you are not your own? For you were bought with a price; therefore, glorify God in your body"* (1 Corinthian 6:19-20, NRSV).

Sometimes sickness results for a very simple reason: we do not take care of ourselves. We sometimes do not heed God's commands and overindulge in food, alcohol, or work. We allow our bodies to run down to where it is susceptible to illness. Doing this is sinful, and thus sickness can be the result of sin.

## SICKNESS CAN RESULT FROM OVERWORK

The scripture teaches that sickness can result from overworking God's ministry. In fact, Paul wrote that a fellow Christian worker, Epaphroditus, was sick to the place of death because of his work for the Lord. We read the following words to the Philippians. *"For he risked his life for the work of Christ, and he was at the point of death while trying to do for me the things you couldn't do because you were far away."* (Philippians 2:30, NLT).

This man of God became sick because he was overworked in the ministry. This is an important warning for those engaged in God's work and busy with their secular jobs. Rest is an essential aspect of work. We find this also to be true in the Old Testament. The prophet

Daniel became ill from the spiritual battle. The vision of the evenings and the mornings told is true. "As for you, seal up the vision, for it refers to many days from now. So, I, Daniel, was overcome and lay sick for some days; then, I arose and went about the king's business. But I was dismayed by the vision and did not understand it" (Daniel 8:26, 27, NRSV).

Daniel became ill due to the spiritual battle in which he was engaged. Believers today can also have this same experience if they do not take care of their bodies.

## JESUS NEEDED REST AND SO DO YOU

We find that Jesus and His apostles needed rest from their labors in the ministry. Mark records the following account. He said to them, *"Come away to a deserted place all by yourselves and rest a while. For many were coming and going, and they had no leisure even to eat"* (Mark 6:31, NRSV). If Jesus and His disciples needed to take some time off from their ministry work, then we ought to do the same. Know that REST IS MINISTRY!

Rest and refreshment are necessary for all humans. There is a time to work, and there is a time to rest. This is crucial for each of us to understand. Indeed, we find that God commanded the people of the nation Israel to rest one day a week. *"It came about on the seventh day that some of the people went out to gather, but they found none. Then the LORD said to Moses, 'How long do you refuse to keep My commandments and My instructions? See, the LORD has given you the sabbath; therefore, He gives you bread for two days on the sixth day. Remain every man in his place; let no man go out of his place on the seventh day' So the people rested on the seventh day"* (Exodus 16, NASB).

## SICKNESS CAN HAVE A SATANIC ORIGIN

There are instances where sickness can originate with the devil. We found this from a statement from Jesus when He healed an infirmed woman.

*"And there was a woman who had had a spirit of infirmity for eighteen years; she was bent over and could not fully straighten herself. And when Jesus saw her, he called her and said to her, 'Woman, you are freed from your infirmity.' And he laid his hands upon her, and immediately she was made straight, and she praised God. But the ruler of the synagogue, indignant because Jesus had healed on the sabbath, said to the people, 'There are six days on which work ought to be done; come on those days and be healed, and not on the sabbath day.' Then the Lord answered him, 'You hypocrites! Does not each of you on the sabbath untie his ox or his ass from the manger, and lead it away to water it? And ought not this woman, a daughter of Abraham whom Satan bound for eighteen years, be loosed from this bond on the sabbath day?'"* (Luke 13:11-16 RSV).

According to Jesus, Satan had bound this woman for eighteen years. When He healed her, the Lord released her from Satan's grip. Therefore, it is possible that some sicknesses may be satanic in origin.

This briefly sums up what the Bible says about where sickness originated and why human beings may become sick. It is important that we have a biblical perspective on the matter. This will allow us to better deal with the subject of sickness and disease whenever they occur and gives us knowledge on how to pray and what to pray against.

## SCRIPTURES CONCERNING HEALING

*"A few days later, when Jesus again entered Capernaum, the people heard that he had come home. They gathered in such large numbers that there was no room left, not even outside the door, and he preached the word to them. Some men came, bringing to him a paralyzed man, carried by four of them. Since they could not get him to Jesus because of the crowd, they made an opening in the roof above Jesus by digging through it and then lowered the mat the man was lying on. When Jesus saw their faith, he said to the paralyzed man, "Son, your sins are forgiven." Now some teachers of the law were sitting there, thinking to themselves, "Why does this fellow talk like that? He's blaspheming! Who can forgive sins but God alone?" Immediately Jesus knew in his spirit that this was what they were thinking in their hearts, and he said to them, "Why are you thinking these things? Which is easier: to say to this paralyzed man, 'Your sins are forgiven,' or to say, 'Get up, take your mat and walk'? But I want you to know that the Son of Man has authority on earth to forgive sins." So he said to the man, "I tell you, get up, take your mat and go home." He got up, took his mat and walked out in full view of them all. This amazed everyone and they praised God, saying, "We have never seen anything like this!" – (Mark 2:1-12, NIV)*

*"One day Peter and John were going up to the temple at the time of prayer—at three in the afternoon. Now a man who was lame from birth was being carried to the temple gate called Beautiful, where he was put every day to beg from those going into the temple courts. When he saw Peter and John about to enter, he asked them for money. Peter looked straight at him, as did John. Then Peter said, "Look at us!" So the man gave them his attention, expecting to get something from them.*

*Then Peter said, "Silver or gold I do not have, but what I do have I give you. In the name of Jesus Christ of Nazareth, walk." Taking him by the right hand, he helped him up, and instantly the man's feet and ankles became strong. He jumped to his feet and began to walk. Then he went with them into the temple courts, walking and jumping, and praising God. When all the people saw him walking and praising God, they recognized him as the same man who used to sit begging at the temple gate called Beautiful, and they were filled with wonder and amazement at what had happened to him." –* (Acts 3:1-10, NIV)

*"Sometime later, Jesus went up to Jerusalem for one of the Jewish festivals. Now there is in Jerusalem near the Sheep Gate a pool, which in Aramaic is called Bethesda and which is surrounded by five covered colonnades. Here a great number of disabled people used to lie—the blind, the lame, the paralyzed. One who was there had been an invalid for thirty-eight years. When Jesus saw him lying there and learned that he had been in this condition for a long time, he asked him, "Do you want to get well?" "Sir," the invalid replied, "I have no one to help me into the pool when the water is stirred. While I am trying to get in, someone else goes down ahead of me." Then Jesus said to him, "Get up! Pick up your mat and walk." At once the man was cured; he picked up his mat and walked." –* (John 5:1-9, NIV)

*"A happy heart makes the face cheerful, but heartache crushes the spirit." –* (Proverbs 15:13, NIV)

*"Hope deferred makes the heart sick, but a longing fulfilled is a tree of life." –* (Proverbs 13:12, NIV)

*"Worship the Lord your God, and his blessing will be on your food and water. I will take away sickness from among you."* (Exodus 23:25, NIV)

*"Dear friend, I pray that you may enjoy good health and that all may go well with you, even as your soul is getting along well."* – (3 John 1:2, NIV)

*"The is what the Lord, the God of your father David, says: 'I have heard your prayer and seen your tears; I will heal you.'"* – (2 Kings 20:5, NIV)

*"He himself bore our sins in his body on the cross, so that we might die to sins and live for righteousness; by his wounds you have been healed."* – (1 Peter 2:24, NIV)

*"Come to me, all you who are weary and burdened, and I will give you rest."* – (Matthew 11:28, NIV)

*"Lord my God, I called to you for help, and you healed me."* – (Psalm 30:2, NIV)

# PROSPERITY IN EVERY AREA OF OUR LIVES

Prayer Focus - Prosperity

*"But remember the Lord your God, for it is he who gives you the ability to produce wealth, and so confirms his covenant, which he swore to your ancestors, as it is today."* – *(Deuteronomy 8:18, NIV)*

Affluence creates influence. Affluence means having a great deal of money and wealthy.

## SEVEN REASONS GOD WANTS US TO PROSPER

### 1. God wants to bless YOU

Psalm 35:27 says, *"Let them shout for joy, and be glad, that favor my righteous cause: yea, let them say continually, Let the Lord be magnified, which hath pleasure in the prosperity of his servant."* God wants your bills paid, needs met, and your family blessed.

Psalm 84:11 in the Amplified Bible says, *"For the Lord God is a Sun and Shield; the Lord bestows [present] grace and favor and [future]* glory (honor, splendor, and heavenly bliss)! No good thing will He with-hold from those who walk uprightly."

God's WORD translation says: "...He does not hold back any blessing..."

Psalm 115:14 in the Amplified Bible says, "May the Lord give you increase more and more, you and your children."

## 2. Jesus came to give us abundant life and not lack

John 10:10 in the New Living Translation says, "The thief's purpose is to steal and kill and destroy. My purpose is to give them a rich and satisfying life."

God's desire is for His children to be rich, not just in spiritual blessings but in material blessings as well.

The King James Version of 2 Corinthians 8:9 says, "For ye know the grace of our Lord Jesus Christ, that, though he was rich, yet for your sakes he became poor, that ye through his poverty might be rich."

There are two different but closely related Greek words for rich in this verse. When the verse says "...though he was rich..." that particular Greek word is plousios which means: "wealthy, abounding in material resources." The second reference to rich is when the scripture says: "...that ye through his poverty might be rich."

This is the Greek word plouteō which means "to be rich, to have abundance; of outward possessions; to be richly supplied; is affluent in resources so that he can give blessings of salvation to all."

The Amplified Bible translation of 2 Corinthians 8:9 says, "For you are becoming progressively acquainted with and recognizing more strongly and clearly the grace of our Lord Jesus Christ (His kindness, His gracious generosity, His undeserved favor and spiritual blessing), [in] that though He was [so very] rich, yet for your sakes He became *[so very] poor, in order that by His poverty you might become enriched (abundantly supplied)."*

## 3. God wants us blessed financially so that we can finance HIS kingdom

Deuteronomy 8:18 in the New International Version says, *"But remember the Lord your God. He gives you the ability to produce wealth. That shows he stands by the terms of his covenant. He promised it with an oath to your people long ago. And he's still faithful to his covenant today."*

First, remember the Lord thy God. Always remember the One who gave you His all so you can be your all through Him. Second, the power to produce wealth is a gift from God. He has endowed you with the seeds of greatness. He has given us the mind of Christ (1 Corinthians 2:16.) Third, God will never give you something unless He expects you to use it. Fourth, God gives us the power to be rich for a reason.

2 Corinthians 8:9 in the New International Version says, *"You know the grace shown by our Lord Jesus Christ. Even though he was rich, he became poor to help you. Because he became poor, you can become rich."*

## 4. God wants us to honor Him with our financial success

Proverbs 3:9-10 in the Amplified Bible says, *"Honor the Lord with your capital and sufficiency [from righteous labors] and with the first fruits of all your income; So shall your storage places be filled with plenty, and your vats shall be overflowing with new wine."*

The Hebrew word for honor is kabad, which means: "Be honorable, be weighty, be rich, be glorious, be burdensome, enjoy honor, be made abundant; to get oneself glory or honor, gain glory." We honor and glorify through our financial success. In reading and re-reading Proverbs 3:9. . .it says honor the Lord with . . .first, your capital and sufficiency [from your righteous labors], otherwise known as your job. But it also says we should honor Him with the first fruits of all our income. . .meaning we should have several or multiple income streams.

## 5. God wants us to be a consistent tithers and givers

Malachi 3:10 in the Amplified Bible says, *"Bring all the tithes (the whole tenth of your income) into the storehouse, that there may be food in My house, and prove Me now by it, says the Lord of hosts, if I will not open the windows of heaven for you and pour you out a blessing, that there shall not be room enough to receive it."* Bring all your tithes, the whole ten percent. If you don't bring the entire ten percent, you are still robbing God. There is no asterisk or conditions at the bottom of the page when we read Malachi 3:10.

The Word of God is not conditional based on the mess or struggle that we may be in, but when we apply the Word of God to our lives it has the power to deliver us from the mess that we have made.

## 6. God wants us to care for the poor, the widows, and orphans

Proverbs 19:17 says, *"He that hath pity upon the poor lendeth unto the Lord; and that which he hath given will he pay him again."*

James 1:27 says, *"External religious worship [religion as it is expressed in outward acts] that is pure and unblemished in the sight of God the Father is this: to visit and help and care for the orphans and widows in their affliction and need, and to keep oneself unspotted and uncontaminated from the world."*

The New Living Translation of James 1:27 says, *"Religion that pleases God the Father must be pure and spotless. You must help needy orphans and widows and not let this world make you evil."*

Exodus 22:22 says, *"Ye shall not afflict any widow, or fatherless child."* The scripture says in Exodus 22:23 that God will know if we don't follow His instructions. "If thou afflict them in any wise, and they cry at all unto me, I will surely hear their cry." Lest there be any mistake, God clearly laid out what the penalty would be for ignoring His instructions.

Exodus 22:24 says, *"And my wrath shall wax hot, and I will kill you with the sword; and your wives shall be widows, and your children fatherless."*

The Message Bible translation of Exodus 22:22-24 says, *"Don't mistreat widows or orphans. If you do and they cry out to me, you can be sure I'll take them most seriously; I'll show my anger and come raging among you with the sword, and your wives will end up widows and your children orphans."* God is serious in His desire for His children to care for the widows and orphans. So, here's the question, can you do more for the poor, the widows, and the orphans when you're poor or prosperous?

## 7. God wants us to be the head and not the tail

Deuteronomy 28:10-13 in the Amplified Bible says: "And all people of the earth shall see that you are called by the name (and in the presence of) the Lord, and they shall be afraid of you." All the people of the earth, not just those in your family, neighborhood, or even your local church.

You can't be a closet Christian and expect to prosper.

*"And the Lord shall make you have a surplus of prosperity, through the fruit of your body, of your livestock, and of your ground, in the land*

*which the Lord swore to your fathers to give you.*" The Lord will give you a surplus of prosperity, not a government stimulus package or an inheritance from a rich relative. Notice the scripture doesn't say He will give you a surplus of poverty. No, He will give you a surplus of prosperity. This verse even shows various ways in which God can get money to you.

"The Lord shall open to you His good treasury, the heavens, to give the rain of your land in its season and bless all the work of your hands; and you shall lend to many nations, but you shall not borrow."

"*And the Lord shall make you the head, and not the tail; and you shall be above only, and you shall not be beneath if you heed the commandments of the Lord your God which I command you this day and are watchful to do them.*"

Yes, in verse 13, we're told to "heed the commandments of the Lord your God," but it's the next six words that should provoke our thinking."

I encourage you to read your Bible and apply the principles to your life. As we begin to prosper, we will more fully understand that affluence creates influence.

---

## SCRIPTURES ABOUT PROSPERITY

---

"*Beloved, I wish above all things that thou mayest prosper and be in health, even as thy soul prospereth.*" – (3 John 2, KJV)

"*A feast is made for laughter, wine makes life merry, and money is the answer for everything.*" – (Ecclesiastes 10:19, NIV)

"*For the love of money is the root of all evil: which while some coveted after, they have erred from the faith, and pierced themselves through with many sorrows.*" – (1 Timothy 6:10, KJV)

*"For it will be like a man going on a journey, who called his servants and entrusted to them his property. To one he gave five talents, to another two, to another one, to each according to his ability. Then he went away. He who had received the five talents went at once and traded with them, and he made five talents more. So also he who had the two talents made two talents more. But he who had received the one talent went and dug in the ground and hid his master's money. Now after a long time the master of those servants came and settled accounts with them. And he who had received the five talents came forward, bringing five talents more, saying, 'Master, you delivered to me five talents; here, I have made five talents more.' His master said to him, 'Well done, good and faithful servant. You have been faithful over a little; I will set you over much. Enter into the joy of your master.' And he also who had the two talents came forward, saying, 'Master, you delivered to me two talents; here, I have made two talents more.' His master said to him, 'Well done, good and faithful servant. You have been faithful over a little; I will set you over much. Enter into the joy of your master.' He also who had received the one talent came forward, saying, 'Master, I knew you to be a hard man, reaping where you did not sow, and gathering where you scattered no seed, so I was afraid, and I went and hid your talent in the ground. Here, you have what is yours.' But his master answered him, 'You wicked and slothful servant! You knew that I reap where I have not sown and gather where I scattered no seed? Then you ought to have invested my money with the bankers, and at my coming I should have received what was my own with interest. So take the talent from him and give it to him who has the ten talents. For to everyone who has will more be given, and he will have an abundance. But from the one who has not, even what he has will be taken away. And cast the worthless servant into the outer darkness. In that place there will be weeping and gnashing of teeth.'"*
(Matthew 25:14-30, ESV)

# PRAYING AGAINST THE SPIRIT OF FEAR!

Prayer Focus - Fear

*"When I am afraid, I put my trust in you."*
– (Psalm 56:3, NIV)

## WHAT IS FEAR?

Fear is one of the most basic human emotions. It is programmed into the nervous system and works like an instinct. We are equipped with the survival instincts necessary to respond with fear when we sense danger or feel unsafe from the time we're infants.

Fear helps protect us. It makes us alert to danger and prepares us to deal with it. Feeling afraid is very natural and helpful. In some situations, fear can be like a warning, a signal that cautions us to be careful.

Like all emotions, fear can be mild, medium, or intense, depending on the situation and the person. A feeling of fear can be brief, or it can last longer.

## HOW FEAR WORKS

When we sense danger, the brain reacts instantly, sending signals that activate the nervous system. This causes physical responses, such as a faster heartbeat, rapid breathing, and increased blood pressure. Blood pumps to muscle groups to prepare the body for physical action (such as running or fighting). Skin sweats to keep the body cool. Some people might notice sensations in the stomach, head, chest, legs, or hands. These physical sensations of fear can be mild or strong.

This response is known as "fight or flight" because that is precisely what the body is preparing itself to do: fight off the danger or run fast to get away. The body stays in this fight-flight state until the brain receives an "all clear" message and turns off the response.

Fear is the word we use to describe our emotional reaction to something that seems dangerous. But the word "fear" is used in another way, too: to name something a person often feels afraid of.

People fear things or situations that make them feel unsafe or unsure. For instance, someone who isn't a strong swimmer might fear deep water. In this case, fear is helpful because it cautions the person to stay safe. Someone could overcome this fear by learning how to swim safely.

Fear can be healthy if it cautions a person to stay safe around something that could be dangerous. But sometimes, fear is unnecessary and causes more caution than the situation demands.

Many people fear speaking in front of others; whether it's giving a report in class, speaking at an assembly, speaking at church, or reciting lines in the school play, speaking in front of others is one of the most common fears people have.

People tend to avoid the situations or things they fear. But this doesn't help them overcome fear; in fact, it can be the reverse. Avoiding something scary reinforces a fear and keeps it strong.

Certain fears are normal during childhood because fear can be a natural reaction to feeling unsure and vulnerable. Young kids often have fears of the dark, being alone, strangers, monsters, or other scary imaginary creatures. School-aged kids might be afraid when it's stormy or at a first sleepover. As they grow and learn, with the support of adults, most kids can slowly conquer these fears and outgrow them.

A spirit of fear is unhealthy. It is consuming and paralyzing.

A spirit of fear is foolish while fearing God is the beginning of wisdom. Where a spirit of fear debilitates, fear of the Lord empowers. When a spirit of fear brings death, the fear of the lord offers life.

---

## SCRIPTURES ABOUT FEAR

---

*"Fear not, for I am with you; be not dismayed, for I am your God; I will strengthen you, I will help you, I will uphold you with my righteous right hand."* – (Isaiah 41:10, ESV)

*"For God gave us a spirit not of fear but of power and love and self-control."* – (2 Timothy 1:7, ESV)

*"Casting all your anxieties on him, because he cares for you."* – (1 Peter 5:7, ESV)

*"When I am afraid, I put my trust in you. In God, whose word I praise, in God I trust; I shall not be afraid. What can flesh do to me?"* – (Psalm 56:3-4, ESV)

*"Of David. The Lord is my light and my salvation; whom shall I fear? The Lord is the stronghold of my life; of whom shall I be afraid?"* – (Psalm 27:1, ESV)

# PRAYING FOR BUSINESS OWNERS AND ENTREPRENEURS

Prayer Focus – Business Owners And Entrepreneurs

*"Lazy hands make for poverty, but diligent hands bring wealth. He who gathers during summer and takes advantage of his opportunities is a son who acts wisely, But he who sleeps during harvest and ignores the moment of opportunity is a son who acts shamefully." –* (Proverbs 10:4-5, NIV)

As Christians, we are always supposed to be at the top of our game because we are representatives of Jesus Christ. Compromising in the workplace and our work ethics in little things is an area that can open doors for the enemy to gain an advantage over us.

Christians are mocked because we do not exemplify a biblical standard in our business lifestyles. How are we to witness and share the gospel of Christ if our work habits are not exemplary? The Bible says that we are living epistles meaning "walking bibles," that are read by all men daily.

I've noticed now more than ever that a lot of the younger generation were not taught proper work habits and now have difficulty holding a job. Our children's messy rooms and lazy, nonchalant attitudes are a symptom of how a generation of parents have neglected to teach their children this truth while they were growing up. We are instructed in Proverbs 22:6 to *"Train up a child in the way he should go: and when he is old, he will not depart from it."* Training involves more than just teaching. The best teachers teach the procedure for doing a job and a set of values for producing that job.

Whatever reasons we give for our neglect in training our children, the truth is we did not take the time needed to train our children properly. We are a world in a hurry, which hinders good workmanship. Laziness and disorganization reflect a lack of caring. We need to teach our children how to do a good job and train them to do their best. Teaching is simply communicating knowledge, while training involves conveying a value system. Good teachers who teach moral values and proper instruction produce quality schooling and the best workers. If we as parents compromise on our lifestyles and work ethics before our children, we communicate those ideas to them.

The Word of God tells us how we can please God in the workplace in Matthew 25:23, *"His lord said unto him, Well done, good and faithful servant; thou hast been faithful over a few things, I will make thee ruler over many things: enter thou into the joy of thy lord."* Being faithful to the little things will encourage us to rule over larger things. The same is true on the negative side; neglecting little things can cause big problems.

As Christians, we must remember that our ministry is to live the Christian life anywhere we are. The most important thing is our relationship with people. We must guard and watch our attitude in the office one toward another as well as our outreach to the people God sends us to be a witness to. Remember the Golden Rule: "Do unto others as you would have them do unto you" (Luke 6:31).

- Ephesians 6:5-9: *"Servants, be obedient to them that are your masters according to the flesh, with fear and trembling, in singleness of your heart, as unto Christ; Not with eyeservice, as menpleasers; but as the servants of Christ, doing the will of God from the heart; With good will doing service, as to the Lord, and not to men: Knowing that whatsoever good thing any man doeth, the same shall he receive of the Lord, whether he be bond or free. And ye masters, do the same things unto them, forbearing threatening: knowing that your Master also is in heaven; neither is there respect of persons with him."*
- Romans 12:10-11: *"Be kindly affectioned one to another with brotherly love; in honour preferring one another; Not slothful in business; fervent in spirit; serving the Lord."*

## THE FIRST EXAMPLE
## OF AN ENTREPRENEUR WAS GOD

*"In the beginning, God created the heavens and the earth. Now the earth was formless and empty, darkness was over the surface of the deep, and the Spirit of God was hovering over the waters. And God said, 'Let there be light,' and there was light."* (Genesis 1:1-3)

The first thing God reveals about Himself in Scripture is not that He is loving, holy, omnipotent, gracious, or just. No, the first thing God shows us is that He is creative. In Genesis, He brings something out of nothing. He brings order out of chaos. He creates for the good of others. In short, God is the first entrepreneur. An entrepreneur is anyone who takes a risk to create something new for the good of others.

Using this definition, the Creator of the universe certainly qualifies as the first entrepreneur. In Genesis, He is clearly creating something new. Before creation, "the earth was formless and empty" until the first entrepreneur spoke. Then, in six days, His voice brought forth the heavens, the earth, light, evening, morning, sky, land, sea, vegetation, sun, moon, stars, animals, and man.

Not only did God create something original, but He also created for the good of others. He added value to people's lives. God doesn't stop revealing His character as creator and entrepreneur in Genesis. The Godhead reveals these characteristics throughout scripture through the Spirit and Son.

## SCRIPTURES ABOUT ENTREPRENEURSHIP

*"Do not love sleep or you will grow poor; stay awake and you will have food to spare."* – (Proverbs 20:13, ESV)

*"You shall remember the Lord your God, for it is he who gives you power to get wealth, that he may confirm his covenant that he swore to your fathers, as it is this day."* – (Deuteronomy 8:18, ESV)

*"Whatever you do, work heartily, as for the Lord and not for men."* – (Colossians 3:23, ESV)

*"And whatever you do, in word or deed, do everything in the name of the Lord Jesus, giving thanks to God the Father through him."* – (Colossians 3:17, ESV)

*"A slack hand causes poverty, but the hand of the diligent makes rich."* – (Proverbs 10:4, ESV)

*"Commit your work to the Lord, and your plans will be established."* – (Proverbs 16:3, ESV)

*"The plans of the diligent lead surely to abundance, but everyone who is hasty comes only to poverty."* – (Proverbs 21:5, ESV)

*"Whatever your hand finds to do, do it with your might, for there is no work or thought or knowledge or wisdom in Sheol, to which you are going."* – (Ecclesiastes 9:10, ESV)

*"Wealth gained hastily will dwindle, but whoever gathers little by little will increase it."* – (Proverbs 13:11, ESV)

*"Do you see a man skillful in his work? He will stand before kings; he will not stand before obscure men."* – (Proverbs 22:29, ESV)

*"It is well with the man who deals generously and lends; who conducts his affairs with justice."* – (Psalm 112:5, ESV)

*"Woe to him who builds his house by unrighteousness, and his upper rooms by injustice, who makes his neighbor serve him for nothing and does not give him his wages."* – (Jeremiah 22:13, ESV)

*"Behold, the wages of the laborers who mowed your fields, which you kept back by fraud, are crying out against you, and the cries of the harvesters have reached the ears of the Lord of hosts."* – (James 5:4, ESV)

*"Whoever oppresses the poor to increase his own wealth, or gives to the rich, will only come to poverty."* – (Proverbs 22:16, ESV)

*"You shall not steal; you shall not deal falsely; you shall not lie to one another."* – (Leviticus 19:11, ESV)

*"Whoever is generous to the poor lends to the Lord, and he will repay him for his deed."* – (Proverbs 19:17, ESV)

*"But seek first the kingdom of God and his righteousness, and all these things will be added to you."* – (Matthew 6:33, ESV)

*"For the Scripture says, 'You shall not muzzle an ox when it treads out the grain,' and, 'The laborer deserves his wages.'"* – (1 Timothy 5:18, ESV)

*"Unequal weights are an abomination to the Lord, and false scales are not good."* – (Proverbs 20:23, ESV)

*"And if you make a sale to your neighbor or buy from your neighbor, you shall not wrong one another."* – (Leviticus 25:14, ESV)

*"You shall do no wrong in judgment, in measures of length or weight or quantity."* – (Leviticus 19:35, ESV)

*"And God is able to make all grace abound to you, so that having all sufficiency in all things at all times, you may abound in every good work."* – (2 Corinthians 9:8, ESV)

*"Whoever works his land will have plenty of bread, but he who follows worthless pursuits lacks sense."* – (Proverbs 12:11, ESV)

*"Pay to all what is owed to them: taxes to whom taxes are owed, revenue to whom revenue is owed, respect to whom respect is owed, honor to whom honor is owed."* – (Romans 13:7, ESV)

*"The integrity of the upright guides them, but the crookedness of the treacherous destroys them."* – (Proverbs 11:3, ESV)

*"Better is a poor man who walks in his integrity than a rich man who is crooked in his ways."* – (Proverbs 28:6, ESV)

*"And the Lord answered me: "Write the vision; make it plain on tablets, so he may run who reads it." – (Habakkuk 2:2)*

*"In all toil there is profit, but mere talk tends only to poverty." –* (Proverbs 14:23)

# PRAYING AGAINST GUILT AND SHAME

Prayer Focus - Freedom From Guilt And Shame

*"And God raised us up with Christ and seated us with him in the heavenly realms in Christ Jesus."* – (Ephesians 2:6, NIV)

Since Christ is free from condemnation before God, so is the sinner who is "in Christ" Not only that, but God has *"raised us up with Christ and seated us with Him in the heavenly realms in Christ Jesus"* (Ephesians 2:6). Being in Christ by faith removes God's condemnation and assures us of eternal life in heaven.

The forgiveness of our sins and the removal of our guilt are only possible because of the incredible loving sacrifice of Jesus Christ. He gave His life to pay the death penalty for us. His shed blood washes away our sins and guilt (1 John 1:7; Revelation 1:5). After we have genuinely repented, we can accept God's forgiveness and not continue to carry guilt, knowing that *"as far as the east is from the west, so far has He removed our transgressions from us"* (Psalm 103:12). We can be blameless in God's eyes and move on with our lives.

*"If we say that we have no sin, we deceive ourselves, and the truth*

*is not in us. If we confess our sins, He is faithful and just to forgive us our sins and to cleanse us from all unrighteousness"* (1 John 1:8-9).

Then we can be completely clean of sin and guilt. As God said through Isaiah, *"Wash yourselves, make yourselves clean; put away the evil of your doings from before My eyes. Cease to do evil, learn to do good; seek justice, rebuke the oppressor; defend the fatherless, and plead for the widow. 'Come now, and let us reason together,' says the LORD, 'though your sins are like scarlet, they shall be white as snow"'* (Isaiah 1:16-18).

## DON'T GIVE SHAME AND GUILT POWER

Shame has plagued us since Adam and Eve bit into the fruit and realized they were naked. Their first instinct was to hide from each other and God (Genesis 3:7–11). They stood guilty before God and were vulnerable to each other and Satan in a whole new horrible way. Suddenly, they were sinful, weak, damaged people living in a dangerous world. They found themselves under God's righteous judgment (Genesis 3:17–19; John 3:19; Romans 6:23), exposed to other sinners' sinful judgment and rejection, and wide-open to the condemning accusations of the evil one (Revelation 12:10).

We also live in this dangerous world and have the same instinct to hide. Because sin is alive in our bodies (Romans 7:23) and because we are beset with weakness (Hebrews 5:2), the kind of shame we often experience is a potent combination of failure and pride. We fail morally (sin), we fail due to our limitations (weakness), and we fail because the creation is subject to futility and doesn't work right (Romans 8:20).

Many people struggle with the fact that they have failed to live up to other people's expectations. Because we are full of pride, we are ashamed of our failures and weaknesses and will go to almost any length to hide them from others. This means pride-fueled shame can have tremendous power over us. It controls significant parts of our lives and consumes precious energy and time in avoiding exposure.

## BREAKING THE POWER OF SHAME

Just because pride moves us to hide our shame in the wrong places doesn't mean our instinct to hide is entirely wrong. It isn't. We need a place to hide, but we need to hide in the right place.

And there is only one place to hide that offers the protection we seek, where all our shame is covered, and we no longer need to fear: the refuge of Jesus Christ (Hebrews 6:18–20). Jesus's death and resurrection are the only remedies for the shame we feel over our grievous sin-failures (Hebrews 9:26). There is nowhere else to go with our sin; there is no other atonement (Acts 4:12). But if we hide in Jesus, He provides us a complete cleansing (1 John 1:9). And when that happens, all God's promises, which find their yes in Christ (2 Corinthians 1:20), become ours if we believe and receive them. And the grace that flows from these promises to us through faith is all-sufficient and abounding and provides for all our other shameful weaknesses and failures (2 Corinthians 9:8).

The key to breaking the power of pride-fueled shame is the superior power of humility-fueled faith in the work of Christ and the promises of Christ. Shame pronounces us guilty and deficient. Jesus pronounces us guiltless and promises that his grace will be sufficient for us in our weaknesses (2 Corinthians 12:9–10). Christ is all (Colossians 3:11). As we trust Jesus as our righteousness (Philippians 3:9) and our provider of everything we need (Philippians 4:19), shame will lose its power over us.

That's what happened to the woman at the well. She listened to Jesus and believed in him; her sin-wrecked life was redeemed and her shame destroyed.

That's what happened to King David. He confessed his sin, repented (2 Samuel 12:13), and trusted the pre-incarnate Christ, and his guilt and shame, which was great, was imputed to Christ and paid for in full.

And that's what happened to the hemorrhaging woman. Jesus did make her tell the crowd about her shame, and in doing so, she received the healing and cleansing she needed. Jesus made her shame a showcase of His grace. And this wonderful experience can also be ours. All it requires is a child-like, wholehearted belief in Jesus (John 14:1).

---

## SCRIPTURES ABOUT GUILT AND SHAME

"If we confess our sins, he is faithful and just to forgive us our sins and to cleanse us from all unrighteousness." Confess whatever is making you feel shame, guilt, and regret." – (1 John 1.9, NIV)

"...he will have compassion upon us; he will subdue our iniquities, and thou wilt cast all their sins into the depths of the sea. Let them go because you have been forgiven." – (Micah 7:19)

"...Christ loved the church and gave himself up for her to make her holy, cleansing her by the washing with water through the word." – (Ephesians 5:25–26)

"There is now no condemnation for those who are in Christ Jesus." – (Romans 8:1)

"Let not your hearts be troubled. Believe in God; believe also in me." – (John 14:1)

*"Awake to righteousness and sin not; for some have not the knowledge of God: I speak this to your shame." – (1 Corinthians 15:34)*

*"Because the Sovereign Lord helps me, I will not be disgraced. Therefore, have I set my face like flint, and I know I will not be put to shame." – (Isaiah 50:7)*

*"Fear not, for you will not be ashamed; be not confounded, for you will not be disgraced; for you will forget the shame of your youth, and the reproach of your widowhood you will remember no more." – (Isaiah 54:4)*

*"No temptation has overtaken you that is not common to man. God is faithful, and he will not let you be tempted beyond your ability, but with the temptation he will also provide the way of escape, that you may be able to endure it." – (1 Corinthians 10:13)*

*"My little children, I am writing these things to you so that you may not sin. But if anyone does sin, we have an advocate with the Father, Jesus Christ the righteous." – (1 John 2:1)*

*"Do not let your hearts be troubled. You believe in God[a]; believe also in me. My Father's house has many rooms; if that were not so, would I have told you that I am going there to prepare a place for you? And if I go and prepare a place for you, I will come back and take you to be with me that you also may be where I am. You know the way to the place where I am going." Thomas said to him, "Lord, we don't know where you are going, so how can we know the way?" Jesus answered, "I am the way and the truth and the life. No one comes to the Father except through me. If you really know me, you will know[b] my Father as well. From now on, you do know him and have seen him." Philip said, "Lord, show us the Father and that will be enough for us." Jesus answered: "Don't you know me, Philip, even after I have been among you such a*

*long time? Anyone who has seen me has seen the Father. How can you say, 'Show us the Father'? Don't you believe that I am in the Father, and that the Father is in me? The words I say to you I do not speak on my own authority. Rather, it is the Father, living in me, who is doing his work. Believe me when I say that I am in the Father and the Father is in me; or at least believe on the evidence of the works themselves. Very truly I tell you, whoever believes in me will do the works I have been doing, and they will do even greater things than these, because I am going to the Father. And I will do whatever you ask in my name, so that the Father may be glorified in the Son. You may ask me for anything in my name, and I will do it." – (John 14:1-14)*

CONSECRATION

# PRAYING FOR IMPACT AND KINGDOM RESULTS

Prayer Focus - Impact And Kingdom Results

*"You are the salt of the earth. But if the salt loses its saltiness, how can it be made salty again? It is no longer good for anything, except to be thrown out and trampled underfoot. You are the light of the world. A town built on a hill cannot be hidden. Neither do people light a lamp and put it under a bowl. Instead, they put it on its stand, and it gives light to everyone in the house. In the same way, let your light shine before others, that they may see your good deeds and glorify your Father in heaven."* – (Matthew 5:13-16, NIV)

Impact means to have a substantial effect on someone or something or the strong effect or influence that something has on a situation or person.

## SCRIPTURES ABOUT IMPACT

*"When Paul and his companions had passed through Amphipolis and Apollonia, they came to Thessalonica, where there was a Jewish*

*synagogue. As was his custom, Paul went into the synagogue, and on three Sabbath days, he reasoned with them from the Scriptures, explaining and proving that the Messiah had to suffer and rise from the dead. "This Jesus I am proclaiming to you is the Messiah," he said. Some of the Jews were persuaded and joined Paul and Silas, as did many God-fearing Greeks and quite a few prominent women. But other Jews were jealous; so they rounded up some bad characters from the marketplace, formed a mob, and started a riot in the city. They rushed to Jason's house in search of Paul and Silas in order to bring them out to the crowd. But when they did not find them, they dragged Jason and some other believers before the city officials, shouting: "These men who have caused trouble all over the world have now come here, and Jason has welcomed them into his house. They are all defying Caesar's decrees, saying that there is another king, one called Jesus." When they heard this, the crowd and the city officials were thrown into turmoil. Then they made Jason and the others post bond and let them go." –* (Acts 17:1-9)

*"And such as do wickedly against the covenant shall he corrupt by flatteries: but the people that do know their God shall be strong, and do exploits." –* (Daniel 11:32)